THE ESTABLISHMENT AND ALL THAT

A collection of major articles
selected from
THE CENTER MAGAZINE
since its beginning
in the Fall of 1967

PUBLISHED BY
THE CENTER FOR THE STUDY OF DEMOCRATIC INSTITUTIONS
SANTA BARBARA, CALIFORNIA

© 1970, THE FUND FOR THE REPUBLIC, INC.

★★★★

An Introduction

From the outset, in 1959, members of the Center for the Study of Democratic Institutions have sought, first, to clarify their own thinking about basic social and political issues and, second, to widen the circles of discussion of these issues through occasional publications, meetings, and conferences. Later it was decided to publish on a regular basis. In the fall of 1967, *The Center Magazine,* a bi-monthly, made its first appearance. Its content was to be drawn largely from papers presented at the Center's almost-daily discussions. This book, a sampling of articles taken from the first two years of *The Center Magazine,* is representative of the Center's activity during that two-year period.

In selecting these articles, the editors were reminded anew that, in the process of clarifying thinking on an issue, one often raises more questions than one answers. This can be annoying in a society which prides itself on demanding, and getting, answers to problems and then moving briskly on to new problems. And, as Socrates discovered, raising questions can be more than annoying, it can be downright dangerous. Nonetheless, those caught up in the dialogue method of self-education willingly run whatever risk is involved in question-asking. They do so knowing that, although we are dependent on others for our *knowledge,* received *wisdom* is a contradiction in terms. The truth that can be called wisdom has to be earned, not received; and it has to be earned by facing up to the toughest questions, those that threaten the very basis of one's position, or conviction, or philosophy, or mythology.

So, this collection of Center-pieces may not be comforting. But we think it may be humanly satisfying. It is, it seems to us, eminently satisfying to wrestle with meaningful problems, with complex issues in which the outcome is of consequence to the human condition. When Denis Goulet, for example, invites us here to consider the dilemma confronting the ethical revolutionary, we are engaged in something more than an intellectual problem-solving exercise; we are caught up in an intensely human issue, the resolution of which must engage all that is noblest and most honorable in the human spirit because it runs ultimately to the meaning of human life and society. What, we might ask ourselves, is more worthy of human effort than this kind of wrestling?

When Peter Marin dares us to plunge into unknown depths of imaginative thinking about the meaning of the now worldwide revolution of youth and its implications for cherished educational institutions and habits, can anything be as uncomfortable a prospect? Or as promising a reward?

It is possible that these articles, here gathered in book form, will sow new seeds of discontent among those not acquainted with the Center's work. We'd like to think that this kind of discontent is healthy if it lends to rational thought and action, to civilized human existence. We hope that this little collection contributes something to that civilization.

THE EDITORS

CONTENTS

Robert M. Hutchins has been trying to bring order out of intellectual chaos all his life. Whether as Dean of the Yale Law School, Chancellor of the University of Chicago, or founder and guiding spirit of the Center, he has been hooked on the idea that the unexamined life is not worth living.

In the interest of clarity and understanding, Hutchins steadfastly rejects cant, obscurity, untested platitudes, and even big words and complex sentences. If the rest of us could match him, this would be a better book. This would also be a better world — at least we would be able to talk to each other.

The Center in the Sixties and Seventies

ROBERT M. HUTCHINS

In 1959 the Board of Directors of the Fund for the Republic established the Center for the Study of Democratic Institutions with a mandate to "clarify the basic issues and widen the circles of discussion about them." The Board's decision followed two years of study that had led to the conclusion that the original purpose of the Fund, to advance understanding of civil liberties and civil rights, could best be carried out in the context of an effort to advance understanding of democratic institutions.

In 1959 the financial future of the Fund was obscure. The Center was perforce made up of part-time consultants, with the staff of the Fund in support. Each of the Center's studies was under the supervision of one or more of the consultants; a member of the staff acted as director of each study. The original projects dealt with the corporation, A. A. Berle, consultant, W. H. Ferry, staff director; the labor union, Clark Kerr, consultant, Paul Jacobs, staff director; war and peace, I. I. Rabi, consultant, Walter Millis, staff director; religious institutions, Reinhold Niebuhr and John Courtney Murray, consultants,

John Cogley, staff director; the mass media, Eric Goldman, and later Harry S. Ashmore, consultants, Frank Kelly, staff director; the political process, Eugene Burdick, consultant, Hallock Hoffman, staff director. George N. Shuster and Harrison Brown were consultants-at-large.

The difficulties of bringing the consultants together led to a gradual shift as the projects on which they worked came to an end. The Center decided to avail itself of the consultants' advice on an individual and ad-hoc basis. Thus the staff became the Center.

The generosity of Chester F. Carlson, who gave the Center almost five million dollars over five years and left it another five million at his death, had a dual effect: it made it possible to foresee a future in which the Center would not be dependent on annual money-raising, and it permitted the Center to take a step that had been debated for many years, expansion of its limited publication program to include a magazine. THE CENTER MAGAZINE has been successful beyond expectations. The one hundred thousand members it has brought the Center have served still further to reduce financial anxiety about the future, and to provide an important national and international audience for the Center's deliberations.

Until the Center has an endowment that relieves it of any conscious or unconscious desire to please and that enables it to deal with any issue as it sees fit, it will not be ideally situated. But the Board of Directors decided in May, 1969, that the organization now had a sufficiently firm and independent basis to enable it to attempt in the nineteen-seventies what it wanted to do in the sixties.

The Board authorized the President to refound the Center according to a procedure in which the Senior Fellows, beginning with the President and one appointed by him, would elect their associates. A total of seven were selected. They will choose others. They are under instructions from the Board to elect the most highly qualified persons to be found.

Harvey Wheeler pointed out in a paper written in 1961 that the early projects of the Center were at that date approaching completion or stalemate. Solutions currently recommended for the problems with which they dealt were seen to be inadequate, because no solutions can be adequate unless they are sought in the widest possible context. Economics and politics, for example, remain unintelligible except in terms of a general conception of social order. The over-arching theme of studies of the social order now has to be the nature of world order and the universe of man in its most fundamental aspects. The Board of Directors last May removed any limitations found in the American background of the Fund for the Republic and any restrictions that might be thought inherent in "the study of democratic institutions." What the Board decided to do was to establish an international community of scholars.

The phrase "community of scholars" is inapplicable in varying degrees to all modern universities. In a recent issue of the *Universities Quarterly,* H. T. Betteridge, of the University of Glasgow, remarks that "learning for its own sake has now become just laughable, for it leads neither to riches nor to power or influence." Academic institutions all over the world are increasingly dedicated to training in narrower and narrower fields of specialization. They can hardly be called intellectual communities, or communities of any kind. The demands upon them by industry and the state have made the university, as the former president of Cornell once boasted, "the great pumping heart" of the industrial state.

The isolation of the specialties is such that there is no way of taming the pretensions of any one of them. One cannot shed light on another, and they cannot come together to focus on the basic or urgent problems of civilization.

The desperate attempts to meet this situation by meetings, conferences, and symposia are laudable but unsuccessful. The problems require systematic and continuous attention, which, by definition, sporadic gatherings cannot give them.

In America academic careerism and foundation funds as well as governmental and industrial grants direct the vast but scattered resources of the multiversity into a network of pipelines leading to the military-industrial complex and other agencies of national power and prosperity.

A recent issue of *Science* reported that one agency, the Air Force Office of Scientific Research, was financing the research of more than a thousand Doctoral candidates and of many more Master's candidates. The report added: "The over-all impact is apparent from the observation that these graduate students rank at the top of the nation's younger generation of scientists and are developing their expertise in areas particularly relevant to Department of Defense interests."

Yet the multiversity may be obsolescent in the sense that the problems lie elsewhere. The revolutions we hear so much about may make the multiversity an anachronism. Nobody can deny the value of discovery and invention, but a most pressing question is how we can live with science and technology. Nobody would care to reduce the prosperity of the advanced industrial nations, but we may be coming to a point at which the issue is not how to produce and distribute goods but how to live human lives, not how to strengthen and enrich the nation-state but how to make the world a decent habitation for mankind. The causes of the present worldwide unrest among students are complicated, but one of them seems to be a growing conviction among young people that contemporary institutions, especially the university, cannot in their present form deal with the dangers and opportunities of the present and future.

Against this background, the Board of Directors of the Center has decided that it is desirable to organize a small center of independent thought and criticism, made up of men and women highly qualified in their specialties who are prepared to devote a major part of their time to a common effort to understand the contemporary world. During the coming year the Center will try to discover whether this can be done. A series of meetings will be held with scholars from all over the world. The present Fellows will seek their advice and their coöperation as resident, visiting, or corresponding members of the Center.

Looking back over the sixties, one can see that the developments are a natural result not only of the improvement in the Center's financial position but also of reflection upon its program. The staff was systematically engaged in such reflection for a year and a half before the Board acted in May. No one who took part in those discussions could escape the conclusion that the academic affairs of the Center should be in the hands of a small number of qualified Senior Fellows. The number should be no larger than might be required to provide a continuing nucleus for the dialogue.

The method of the dialogue, though difficult, was seen to be the only one that encouraged the kind of interdisciplinary criticism in which the Center has been engaged. The dialogue had to be about subjects selected by the participants. It had to be frequent enough to build up continuity — meetings should not be so far apart that what went on in one was forgotten by the time the next took place. On the other hand, the dialogue had to be infrequent enough to permit the participants to prepare and at the same time to get on with their own studies. These studies would be the basis of later meetings led by them.

Frequent, but not too frequent, dialogue on subjects chosen by the group, accompanied by work of one's own that was to be brought ultimately to the table — this was the method that was carried to some degree of perfection by the Center and that will be employed by the refounded organization.

Center Fellows, and often visitors as well, soon get out of the habit of referring to themselves as lawyers or political scientists or whatever they happen to be. They talk to the problem under consideration, bringing their own special knowledge to bear on it, at the same time recognizing that no single discipline can have the final word on the kind of issue with which the Center deals. For example, the last discussion in June of this year took place with Arthur Jensen, Professor of Educational Psychology, University of California at Berkeley, on the inheritance of intelligence. The staff had had three previous meetings on Professor Jensen's views, one of them with him. The final conference on the topic was attended by two visiting political scientists and a visiting psychologist. The question of the inheritability of intelligence as set forth by Professor Jensen in the *Harvard Educational Review* has become a *cause célèbre* in the academic world; subsequent issues of the *Review* are devoted entirely to critiques of Jensen's thesis and to his reply. These scholarly exchanges have spilled over into allegations of latent racism and angry charges that Jensen's researches support the anti-integration political faction outside the academy. The controversy has spread to include the methods and responsibilities of scientists; the proportions are approaching those of the great Lysenko imbroglio that divided the academic community in the Soviet Union a few years ago.

If the Jensen affair has attracted so much attention, it might be asked what special contribution the Center can make to the discussion. The answer lies in the central thesis of the Center, that it is impossible to explore such issues within the limits of a single academic discipline, or a cluster of related disciplines. Professor Jensen has raised prime questions of psychology that must be dealt with by specialists, but attending them are grave matters of public policy for which the same specialists may have no particular competence. It is the Center's contribution to take the discussion into multi-disciplinary territory, and to insist that the issues must be appraised finally in terms of human values. We believe the same thing is true of most of the major issues that confront mankind.

ৼ

The work of the Center has shown that all these issues are interrelated. Whether we think of how to live with science and technology or how to advance the idea of world community or to remedy the economic disparities that plague the world, we notice at once that, though solid work must be done by all the disciplines bearing on the problem, there must also be some way of bringing them together if the issue is to be seen in the round, without distortion.

Rexford G. Tugwell's new constitution for the United States is now in its thirty-fourth draft. The Center entered upon this project without any notion that the eventual document might be considered by the people. The Center's intention was to use these constitutional drafts as a focus for its work, to give concreteness to its speculations, and to force it to think carefully about the kind of charter a modern democracy ought to have. Now I am not so sure. If the present demand for a constitutional convention persists, it may be well to have before the country a carefully worked out plan to which those interested in freedom and justice can repair. The motives of those who are urging a convention seem to have little to do with freedom and justice.

The Tugwell study of the Constitution has to embrace all the new conditions and considerations that characterize the new world. It would obviously be absurd to have it criticized by constitutional lawyers alone, for they are frequently unfamiliar with the conditions with which a constitution must deal. By the time Governor Tugwell's final draft is published it will have been inspected from every point of view by experts in all the fields that it impinges upon.

So it is with the problem of world organization, which overlaps the question of controlling technology, that of economic development, and even that of the American Constitution, for America is the most powerful country in the world. Wherever this problem is touched, it immediately calls for the collaboration of specialists.

The seabed, for example, once thought to be the common property of mankind, now appears to have economic and military value. Only a coöperative effort by statesmen, businessmen, and scholars in many fields can lead to a political framework in which the interests of the peoples of the world can be safeguarded. Elisabeth Mann Borgese's project on world organization, which can be traced back to the world constitution framed by a committee at the University of Chicago in 1947, is closely linked to the struggle for the seabed. Officers of and ambassadors to the United Nations have recognized the importance of this work and have assisted in making plans for an international meeting to be held in Malta in 1970, at which a program for a regime of the sea will be presented and discussed.

Throughout the last decade the Center has been concerned with science and technology. An Occasional Paper by Donald Michael on cybernation, published by the Center in 1962, was an attempt to indicate the nature and consequences of the technological revolution. A number of international conferences have been held at the Center on this subject since that date and many publications have resulted from them. A continuing study under the direction of Harvey Wheeler is called the Constitutionalization of Science; it is concerned with the control of the applications of science in the public interest. While the advanced nations have been turning their attention to other planets, this one is being made uninhabitable by the unexpected side effects of scientific progress. The problem now is literally how to save the world. What is going on in the seabed is an example of what may happen, and the relationship of this study to the others is clear. It is also clear that no system for the control of the applications of science can be devised without the type of collaboration among the disciplines that is characteristic of the Center's work.

Building on the studies of war and peace conducted in its early days, the Center in 1964 decided to arrange a convocation to call attention to the papal encyclical *Pacem in Terris,* a document that seemed to suggest paths toward peaceful coexistence among men of different nations and ideologies. The object was to see whether the understanding and interchange advocated by Pope John XXIII was possible. Two thousand people from many countries assembled in New York, and interchange between East and West did occur. The addresses of the representatives of what was then called the Soviet bloc were conciliatory. Positions that had seemed fixed became less rigid. The meeting showed that East-West dialogue could take place.

Encouraged by this result, the Center held another meeting, Pacem in Terris II, for three hundred and fifty invited guests in Geneva in 1967. The effort was to broaden the dialogue. In one way it conspicuously failed, for the Soviet Union, citizens of which had eagerly coöperated in plans for the meeting, withdrew at the last minute because of the war in Vietnam, and many Arab representatives declined or disappeared because of the Six Day War with Israel. From many other points of view, on balance, the meeting succeeded — the Germans, East and West, discussed in public for the first time their points of difference and agreement; the countries of Southeast Asia came together to request a conference among themselves looking toward the neutralization of the region; and many public persons speaking in a private capacity discussed the international relations of their countries with surprising candor.

The virtue of the kind of private peacemaking in which the Center has engaged lies in its flexibility. When public positions are frozen, private groups can establish private relations that may influence public attitudes. When representatives of the Southeast Asian countries asked the Center to invite them to a conference under its auspices, the Center put the natural question, why do you need us? The reply was that the official relations among these nations were such that no one of them could take the initiative.

In private meetings under private auspices, where everybody is speaking in his private capacity, plans can be put forward that a government would hesitate to present because they might be thought signs of weakness. It is a rule of official diplomacy that one must always seem to be negotiating from strength. Hence the difficulties of the U.N., an organization of sovereign states. Having undertaken to formulate a program for the seabed, and having assembled a large committee for this purpose, the U.N. finds itself unable to move. Meanwhile, the member states with access to the oceans are proceeding to stake out their claims.

The risk in private peacemaking is considerable. Although the Center has never made a move of this kind without the knowledge of the government of the United States, it has not been able to count on the sustained support of that government, even when such support has been promised. For example, during the planning for Pacem in Terris II, the Soviet delegation proposed that the Center try to see what private peacemaking could accomplish with regard to the war in Vietnam. With the concurrence of the State Department, the Center established connections with Hanoi; Harry S. Ashmore and William Baggs, with Luis Quintanilla, an experienced Mexican diplomat and consultant to the Center, went there. Discussions with Ho Chi Minh and other North Vietnamese officials were so promising that Ashmore and

Baggs returned for a second visit. Significant proposals did emerge. However, confusion in the State Department and the White House rendered these overtures abortive. The story is told in the special Center Report by Ashmore and Baggs, *Mission to Hanoi.*

The Center does seem to have a certain attraction for those who see places where private peacemaking might work. I have already mentioned the instance of the crisis about the ocean bottom. Another example is that of American-Japanese-Chinese relations. Through Harrop Freeman, Professor of Law at Cornell and a consultant to the Center, a group in the Liberal Party of Japan approached the Center with a request for a conference in Santa Barbara about the policy the United States and Japan should adopt toward Communist China. Ten leaders of the Japanese group attended the meeting, held in January, 1969. The Center invited four leading U.S. senators of both parties and other public figures and experts on the Far East. The exploration of the issues was as thorough as time permitted. The Japanese indicated satisfaction with the results and have suggested further conferences in Tokyo to which they would invite citizens of mainland China.

The project known as the Civilization of the Dialogue, under the direction of John Wilkinson, carries private peacemaking to a more profound level. It is an attempt to understand the conditions of cross-cultural, international, and inter-ideological communication and to test that understanding by efforts at intellectual coöperation. Relations have been established with the *Neues Forum* group in Vienna, which has many connections with individuals and groups in the Soviet Union and other countries in eastern Europe. Professor Fred Warner Neal, a consultant to the Center, has been helpful in putting the Center in touch with scholars in the Soviet Union and eastern Europe. A steady stream of these scholars has flowed through the Center. There is a Rumanian Visiting Fellow, Ileana Marculescu, now in residence, and Academician N. Inozemtsev, a Russian social scientist, is a consultant. Joint publishing arrangements have been made with the *Neues Forum* group and with the Institute of American Studies in Moscow.

ۥ

At the rate of about four meetings a week throughout the calendar year for a decade the Center has touched upon the major issues that have arisen or that seem likely to arise in the contemporary world. Some of them, as I have indicated, it has selected for continued study. Others it has dealt with more summarily, thinking that it has made its contribution by calling attention to them. Where it has felt that novel or heretical views deserved consideration it has not hesitated to provide a forum for them. For this reason the Center has had some utility as an early-warning system.

Its first projects adumbrated the course the organizations under study— religious institutions, the corporations, the mass media, and the unions — might take or ought to take. As long ago as 1958 a paper written by John Graham and published by the Center recommended that conscription be abolished, and added that if this recommendation could not be adopted, selection should be by lot. These suggestions are now a commonplace of political discussion.

A symposium on the Negro as an American, which was conducted in 1963, one on a free press and a fair trial in 1965, one on the opinions and aims of radical youth in 1967, and one in 1967 in which the present Chief Justice set forth somewhat unorthodox views of the administration of criminal justice illustrate the value of an independent institution bent on trying to discover and understand what is going on in the world. I could extend this list almost indefinitely to include, for example, the city, the university, bureaucracy, ecology, and ghetto education.

In general, the Center has tried to avoid the burning issues because by definition they are already receiving attention. The Center has thought its main function was to bring to the surface those issues which had not yet come to public notice but which seemed likely to become the burning issues of the future. The Center has not tried to tell people what to think; it has on occasion ventured to suggest what they ought to be thinking about. It has also on occasion, where it has thought that a fair presentation of all sides of a burning issue was unlikely, arranged for such a presentation. The most recent example is the Occasional Paper on the anti-ballistic missile, which preceded the public controversy.

As the first ten years of the Center draws to a close, as one era ends and another begins, I look back with some satisfaction at the successful attempt to found a center of independent thought and criticism, to learn how to gain comprehension through dialogue, to clarify the basic issues — and some burning ones — and widen the circles of discussion about them. I am grateful to all the colleagues and collaborators who have brought the Center to its present distinction and to all the friends, members, and supporters who have made their work possible. I am confident that by building on its experience the Center will go from strength to strength in the next decade. ❧

The Establishment and All That

Joseph P. Lyford interviewed by John Cogley

Q: *About six years ago, you began research on what ultimately became* The Airtight Cage, *a study of urban life on the West Side of New York. What were its themes?*

LYFORD: The main one was the life of a mixed community in an area where Negroes, Puerto Ricans, and middle-class whites are thrown together — how they manage their problems, especially problems connected with schooling, housing, health, welfare, and politics.

Q: In the two years since the book was published there have been many developments. The student revolt, the black revolt, the New Politics, various other manifestations, all indicate that the concern you felt is now widespread. The vague villain in all these present protests is the capital E Establishment. Do you agree?

LYFORD: I think we are constantly moving from one stereotype notion about our life to another. The Establishment talk has tended to create one more oversimplified picture of our situation. Suddenly everybody in suburbia or the white middle class in the city has become the villain. The assumption by some militant people in the black power movement seems to be that the only reason things are not changing is because white middle-class people in the suburbs are not bestirring themselves. This is a serious mistake, I think. It assumes that if people are middle-class and white, they exercise real control over their system. It has become apparent to me, on the contrary, and to many other persons with middle-class backgrounds who have attempted to influence the course of political or social affairs, that we are equally powerless to effect change. The System is out of control for us, too. We just cannot control what is happening in our own communities — the plight of the schools, the alienation of our children, our inability to effect changes in the attitude of the United States Congress.

Q: The way you are talking it seems impossible for anyone working within to do anything about The System — or at least it is very difficult. The argument of those in the black revolt, and to some extent of persons in the New Politics movement, is no different. They are attacking The System more than people, they say. Their basic objection to those who supposedly make up the Establishment is that such people uphold and sustain The System.

LYFORD: There are certain impersonal forces over which all individuals are gradually losing control. I think that it's reached the point where *subsystems,* rather than people, even Establishment people, uphold The System. For example, the corporation, and especially those corporations involved with the military complex in this country, no longer seem to be under personal control. In the past I suppose you could say that Human beings were the victims of the machine. Today, though, we are victims of a very different sort of systematic procedure. I don't mean that there are no people involved, but who knows who actually makes the decisions in the corporations that in turn, through pressures, affect congressional policies, budgets, and war programs?

Q: You would agree, then, that the students practicing the politics of disruption in the universities or the militant black-power leaders who consider themselves in full revolt are on the right track. In other words, you would not identify your position with a reform movement so much as with a total revolutionary movement.

LYFORD: That's right. One of my criticisms of the civil-rights movement in the past was that it wasn't really revolutionary. It was somehow an attempt through integration and other proceures to effect some sort of superficial accommodation. I have long believed that very radical changes have to be made. In *The Airtight Cage* I talked about bringing society to a halt, paralyzing its ability to function, if necessary. If you can't change the manner in which The System is functioning, at least you can turn off the current. I am disturbed, to be sure, as I think many old-fashioned civil libertarians are, by some of the details of the students' revolt. I don't like the idea of Columbia students going in and rifling filing cases and swiping letters and reading them in public. I don't like violence, whether it is carried out by students or police. But violent reactions against The System are only to be expected when it frustrates necessary changes.

Q: Usually when people talk about The System, it is left amorphous and vague. Nevertheless, you seem to feel there is a malaise throughout the society — a kind of disillusionment even with what we thought were our best values. There is, for example, the widespread disenchantment with liberalism. I notice the anger of the young is turned more often toward the liberal establishment than toward any conservative establishment. These days nobody gets nearly as angry with "Wall Street" as with corporate liberalism, as it is called. Has liberalism, too, become establishmentarian, a tool of The System?

LYFORD: I think so. The revolt of young people against traditional liberalism, however, is based on the mistaken assumption that the liberal is really a mover and shaker in society. The liberal, to be sure, believed in the democratic process, the ability of the individual to make himself felt by personal effort. This, though, has proven to be false. The liberal has been repeatedly defeated in these efforts.

Q: By whom?

LYFORD: He has been defeated by political procedures and organizational politics, which go on regardless. While the liberal acts as an individual, operating on a set of political principles, his adversary is very often an impersonal economic institution, governed by managers, without any regard to political principle. This forms part of the present disenchantment with liberalism. It is based upon young people's assumption that the liberal had the power to succeed, and failed. I am sure I contributed as an individual to the disenchantment by making some early idealistic observations about the power of the citizen to alter his environment through individual political action.

There is also another aspect. That is the question of the manner in which our political process has come to be dominated by the technological. The technology of our society today is so complex that it is beyond the power of individuals to cope with it, or even understand it. Anybody who has ever dealt with a government bureaucracy knows that there is an enormous difference between the views held by the individuals who run it and what the bureaucracy as an institution does despite the wishes of everybody in it. And here, once more, the old liberal presumption that we are a society based upon participational democratic procedures has turned out to be an illusion. Again the liberal comes in for attack.

There is still another aspect. When frustrations have built up to the point of irrational explosion, people get hurt in the process — innocent black people, innocent white people, innocent policemen, innocent civic leaders. The traditional liberal, then, often enough is still clinging to a concern for personal liberties and respect for personal rights, and so you find him in the middle between the disrupters and the forces of "law and order." He finds that while he may be sympathizing with the general purpose of the radicals he is appalled by what he sees happening to the individual in the course of the struggle.

Q: Do you think there is really an identifiable Establishment? Is it simply people who uphold The System we are talking about? Or is the Establishment another word for The System itself?

LYFORD: They are probably synonymous. It is what makes you feel powerless in your personal efforts to achieve your own ideals for society. This means that it is not any one group of persons or any one thing. It is a system that frustrates every individual — regardless of his politics — who is attempting to deal with it. For example, the person in the suburb who talks about his private property, and how he doesn't want things taken away from him, is just as much a victim of this sense of powerlessness and fear as anybody else. And, of course, when you have this sense of powerlessness, it is natural to assume that you feel it because somebody, you don't know who, has taken power away from you.

Q: One of the things one notices is that the revolt, the malaise, whatever you want to call it, is found all over the world. It seems to be popping up everywhere.

The behavior of students in Poland and Germany isn't a great deal different from the behavior of students in New York or Paris. The disenchantment, in fact, seems to transcend political systems and ideological differences.

LYFORD: I think that what bothers young people the world over, whether they know it or not, is immorality. They may not even understand what The System is or how it got that way, but wherever they look they see frightful social immorality. This cannot but produce in any young person a feeling of revulsion. I think it affects all of us, subconsciously or otherwise. Our society, for example, devotes huge amounts of its gross national product — and I really mean gross — to overconsumption, and at the same time it grinds up children into little pieces.

Q: Would you include all kinds of nations, living under quite different political systems, in this general charge that the young are revolted by the social immorality they see?

LYFORD: Regardless of the difference in development of countries throughout the world, or the difference in their racial populations, or the ideology they subscribe to, there is an instinctive outrage against the breakdown of old arrangements. Whether a society is attempting to deal with hunger, disease, or war, they don't feel they are progressing with hope for the future. Today in some way or other peoples the world over are subject to this paralysis and breakdown.

Q: Some people would say that the enemy common to men living under these various political systems, whether the communist, the capitalist, or any other, is what might be summed up as modernity. In other words, it is the complex of technology and bureaucracy ,that is found in Warsaw just as it is found in New York.

26

LYFORD: I would go even further than that and say that even the so-called underdeveloped countries, which are in a relatively primitive state and have not been deeply affected by modern culture or technology, are similarly afflicted. Modernity also affects them, in the sense that they are condemned to be part of the world technology. It is thwarting them even in the early stages of their development.

Q: What are your views of the student revolt? I know that you are not an uncritical supporter. At the same time I think you have a basic sympathy with the aims and goals of the politics of disruption, as it is called.

LYFORD: I think maybe the best way to describe my feelings is to describe the views of a friend who is a professor at Columbia. We were both put off by some of the things that happened there. I don't happen to believe that the police were the only villains in the situation. I was appalled by some of the disruption — students trespassing on the rights of other students, for example. Individual rights were trampled on by both sides.

Q: Is that a liberal hang-over, for you to have such a concern?

LYFORD: I think so. I don't think I'll ever get over it, either, because I lived through the Joe McCarthy days and got to be very sensitive about the rights of other people, whether I agreed with them or not.

This professor friend of mine, who felt the same way, said, "We've got to recognize that in doing this to Columbia at least the students are giving us a chance to get in there and do things about this University that have needed to be done for a long time." He said, 'Let's, for instance, tear open this phony Pulitzer Prize Committee, and make it something with a real meaning." And he enumerated a whole list of other things that didn't have anything to do with that gymnasium in Morningside Park, which supposedly started the student revolt. This is also the way I feel. I'm split, then, in my attitude toward the students.

Q: Students who are leading the revolts often seem to have a cavalier view of personal rights, reasoning that their cause is bigger than the claims of individuals. In the past we may have often ignored individual rights, but we didn't feel easy about justifying it. Now I've discovered in talking to some younger people that they think it's almost sheer sentimentality to be overly concerned with such matters. Such a concern, some say, is another vestige of the ineffectual liberalism they are revolting against.

LYFORD: I feel that the students who express this view are actually totalitarian in spirit. The fact that they have a crusading fervor or zeal or a passion about their cause no more entitles them to trample on other people than it exculpated the people who sincerely believed in what Joe McCarthy was doing and said the end justified McCarthy's means. For example — and I'm speaking as a dove — I do not agree that somebody who is disturbed about the war in Vietnam has a right to prevent another student from being interviewed by a recruiter from Dow Chemical. I like to see students picket the recruiting station. I'm for that. But I think that a student who wants to go in for an interview with Dow representatives has a right to do so.

Q: Do you think that Dow Chemical has a right to recruit on the campus?

LYFORD: That is a separate issue. Dow does have a right under the regulations of the University to recruit. Whether this is desirable is another question. But the problem is not solved by physically forcing persons away from the door. I'm also very much out of sympathy with professors who will shut down a class in sympathy with a boycott. I feel that any student who wants to boycott a class has a right to do so. I won't penalize him as long as he gets his work done. But I also feel I have a responsibility to see that any student who wants to come to my class can do so.

Q: I wonder if the struggle against violence is simply a lost cause. It is interesting that some of the most vigorous opponents of the Vietnam war are encouraging — and not only encouraging but justifying and even advocating — the use of violence to solve problems at home.

LYFORD: That is probably true in some cases, but I also think that a lot of the feeling about the extent to which violence is subscribed to by the student Left, by the militant black community, and by some militants in the white community has often been exaggerated. The exaggeration is a by-product of the way the press has reported on such matters. The black community in this country is composed by and large of people who do not believe in violence and hold very strongly that there is no answer to our problems today except through peaceful resolution, by militant social action but not violence. I think they show considerably more maturity than some of the more articulate people we read about in the press or see on television proclaiming that "authorized" violence is the answer to America's problems at home and abroad.

The Other America Revisited

MICHAEL HARRINGTON

The Other America was published in March, 1962. Now, almost seven years later, the condition that book described is objectively not quite as evil as it was; politically and morally, it is worse than ever. For despite a long, federally induced boom and an "unconditional" war on poverty, tens of millions of Americans still live in a social underworld and an even larger number are only one recession, one illness, one accident removed from it.

Ironically, perhaps the most dramatic single breakthrough of the government's anti-poverty effort is the increase in our official knowledge of the needless suffering that we tolerate. President Johnson's program did not achieve full employment for all nor provide impoverished children and aging people with an income but it did generate a tremendous amount of research, seminars, discussions, and even mass-media reports. So, since the poor have become less invisible, for we know they are there, the society has become even more guilty; now it knows its callousness.

Revisiting the other America in 1969 is easier than going there in the late fifties and early sixties. Now Washington has produced some revealing maps of misery. In general, the official figures show some progress in eliminating poverty, but the accomplishment is so modest that one economic downturn would annul it — and the powerful voices urging a calculated increase in unemployment so that the price stability of the affluent can be protected would bring just such a downturn. Even if that does not come to pass, there is a disturbing potential in the other America of 1969 that particularly menaces both the young and the black poor. In looking at these trends statistically, one must remember that, even though the definitions and the percentages are much more precise than in 1962, there is an enormous margin of error which usually favors understatement and over-optimism. Not very long ago, the government triumphantly announced that there had been a major decrease in deteriorated housing. Then in the summer of 1967 it turned out that the gains had actually been negligible or even nonexistent; and in the 1968 Report of the Council of Economic Advisers the Administration admitted that housing deterioration in big-city slums had actually increased. These inaccuracies were not the result of a conscious attempt to delude. They were honest mistakes — but they were often seized upon by those who want to minimize the problem of poverty in America.

More generally there is a real invisibility of the poor. The Bureau of the Census has only recently discovered that it had not counted a significant minority of the adult Negro males in the ghetto. Some years before this acknowledgment, Bayard Rustin had told me that there were more blacks in America than the government figured. He pointed out that there were special problems in a place like Harlem — for instance, people doubling-up in apartments, a fair number of individuals who feared any contact with The Man, even with the census-taker — which could lead the professionals to err. I thought that Rustin had created an amateur's fantasy until the hard data began to come in (for instance, the 1967 Manpower Report of the Department of Labor found an "undercount" of twenty per cent of the adult men in the slums). This means that there are several million Americans whose conditions of life are so mercurial that they do not even qualify to be a statistic.

With this understanding that the government's numbers are too sanguine, we should take a closer look at them. One of the most imaginative students of the "poverty line" is Mollie Orshansky of the Department of Health, Education, and Welfare. For some time now rightists, like William F. Buckley, Jr., have tried to discredit concern for the poor by arguing that all of the definitions are totally subjective and relative. There is unquestionably an historic element in the setting of such standards — hungry Americans are certainly better off than starving Indians — but it is Miss Orshansky's merit that she emphasizes the objective determinants of misery in the other America. She takes the Department of Agriculture's low-cost diet plan ($5.90 a week for a four-person family in January, 1964) and the "economy" plan (for "temporary or emergency use when funds are low" at $4.60 a week, or twenty-two cents per meal per person, in January, 1964) and puts them at the center of an imagined budget. Neither diet guarantees adequacy, but if a family falls below them it is certain that they will miss important nutrients.

Miss Orshansky then worked out the rest of the poverty budgets in relation to these food costs. In this way, anyone who falls below the poverty line will have less than a minimum diet for health or, more generally, will have to choose between necessities. (The 1968 Report of the Citizens' Board of Inquiry into Hunger and Malnutrition in the United States concluded that "malnutrition among the poor has risen sharply over the past decade.") Using the Orshansky approach, the Social Security Administration came up with a figure of $3,130 for an urban family of four as the upper limit of impoverishment.

By 1966, the poverty line had risen to $3,335. (While this index went up by nine per cent, the average income of four-person families in America had increased by thirty-seven per cent, so the new criterion meant that the poor had even less of a share of affluence.) As a result, 17.8 per cent of the people were under the line in 1966 as compared to twenty-four per cent in 1959. This statistic allows the celebrators of America to claim that the other America is disappearing at a reasonable rate. It is that claim which I want to challenge here.

There is no point in denying that there has been some progress. We are now in the seventh year of an unprecedented prosperity which was purchased, in considerable measure, with a twenty-billion-dollar tax subsidy that disproportionately favored the rich individuals and corporations. At the same time, the official unemployment figures have been reduced to under four per cent — but have not gone down to the three per cent goal that John F. Kennedy set as the mark of "full employment" when he became

President. The first several years of this boom did not aid the unskilled workers and the hard-core unemployed, although eventually a few of the crumbs of good times trickled down to them.

Pride, in short, must be somewhat restrained. The poverty line, is, after all, an artificial, if extremely useful, construct. Miss Orshansky herself has pointed out that millions hover just above the definition (Daniel Patrick Moynihan calls them the "at risk" population). In 1966, there were more than three million families with incomes between $3,000 and $4,000; most of them were not officially classified as poor but all of them were in danger of becoming so with one bad break in the national economy or in their private lives.

Indeed, as Robert C. Wood of the Department of Housing and Urban Development has pointed out, the "average" American who works and earns between $5,000 and $10,000 a year "owes plenty in installment debts on his car and appliances. He finds his tax burden heavy, his neighborhood services poor, his national image tarnished, and his political clout diminishing. This, too, is alienation." And the Bureau of Labor Statistics said that, in late 1966, it took $9,191 a year for a four-person urban family to maintain a "moderate standard of living." If life for the organized, theoretically well-paid working class is still this precarious, one is probably justified in including as well all Americans in 1969 with family incomes (for four, in a city) of less than $5,000 within the magnetic field of poverty. This has explosive implications if the proposal of the top corporate executives to "trade off" an unemployment increase for an inflation decrease are put into action. It also means that the ambiance, if not the precise dimensions, of the other America has changed little since

1962 even though the society has produced unprecedented wealth.

In two particularly tragic cases it is not necessary to speculate about the numbers. The children and the blacks among the poor are worse off than when the war on poverty began. "All told," writes Mollie Orshansky, "even in 1966, after a continued run of prosperity and steadily rising family income, one-fourth of the nation's children were in families living in poverty or hovering just above the poverty line." This fact, of course, has the most disturbing and dangerous implications for the future. On the one hand, poverty more and more becomes a fate because the educational, economic, and social disadvantages of life at the bottom become progressively more damaging; and, on the other hand, the poor still have more children than any other group. Present evidence points to the melancholy conclusion that the twenty-five per cent of the young who are poor, or near-poor, will have large families very much like the ones of which they are now members. If this is true, the current incidence of poverty among children will guarantee that, short of radical political decisions, the next generation in the other America will be even more numerous than this one.

With Negroes, the problem is more a relative position than an absolute increase in indignity, but this is still a politically explosive fact. In 1959 the Social Security Administration fixed the black percentage of the other Americans at twenty-five per cent; by 1966, the proportion had risen to thirty-three per cent. This, of course, still shows that the scandal of poverty actually afflicts more whites than blacks, but it also indicates that discrimination even applies to the rate at which people escape from beneath the poverty line. During these years of prosperity even the worst off of the white Americans have had a special advantage, compared to the Negroes.

It is important to add to this brief survey of the federally certified dimensions of needless economic and social suffering in this country the remarkable "sub-employment" index of the Department of Labor. The index was developed in order to get a more accurate picture of the working — and non-working — lives of people in the slums. Whereas the official definition of unemployment, which currently is fixed at about 3.5 per cent for the nation as a whole, only counts those who are out of work and looking for work, the notion of sub-employment is much more comprehensive. It gives weight to part-time unemployment, to the fact that many people have to toil for poverty wages, to the twenty per cent of the "invisibles" in the slums, and to those who do not look for a job because they are sure they will not find one.

On this basis, the Labor Department discovered sub-employment rates in November, 1966, that ranged from around thirty per cent in the New York ghettos to near fifty per cent in New Orleans. The full significance of this analysis did not become apparent until the winter of 1967 and the report of the National Commission on Civil Disorders. For it was then that the nation learned that the typical rioter was not the least educated, most impoverished, and chronically unemployed citizen of the ghetto. Rather, he was a high-school dropout and a teen-ager and he had worked — but at a menial job. In other words, the frustrations of sub-employment — most particularly of laboring long hard hours without any real hope of advancement — are perhaps more likely to incite a man to violence than the simple despair of having no job at all.

To sum up — by courtesy of the government's

card file (and computer tapes) on outrages in this nation — there has been modest progress in the official figures: a drop in the poverty population from twenty-five per cent to around eighteen per cent. Nevertheless, those who crossed the lines are still very close to the world hunger and hovels. There are signs that the present-day children of the poor will become the parents of even poorer children in the immediate future. Black Americans are falling further and further behind the whites. And the sub-employment statistics indicate a depression while the official jobless rates are cited to show that there is full employment.

What of the quality of life among the poor? Here, I think, the reality is more optimistic, but it is very easy to visualize a reversal of the positive trends.

The war on poverty was never more than a skirmish and the provisions for "maximum feasible participation of the poor" were quickly subverted by hysterical mayors. In theory, the country wants the disadvantaged to stand up and fight for their rights as all the immigrants groups did; in practice, we have knocked people down for taking that pious myth seriously. And yet, there has been a significant growth in local insurgency. It was given an impetus, a public legitimacy, by the anti-poverty efforts of recent years. To a degree, then, the other America has become less passive and defeated, more assertive. This is an enormous gain, for it is the psychological precondition for political and economic advance.

In saying this, I do not wish to suggest for a moment that the poor constitute a latter-day proletariat in the socialist sense of the term (a group goaded to solidarity and struggle by the common conditions of working life). Romantics who held such a theory have been shocked by the seemingly low rates of participation in various community elections. The industrial plant, which assembles large groups of people under a single discipline and with similar grievances about wages and working conditions, is very different from a slum. The company and its assembly line provide an institutional spine for union organizers, but in the world of the tenements there is no such unifying experience and people turn upon one another more than they join together. As the President's Crime Commission reported, the main victims of violence by the black poor were the black poor.

Once this crucial point is understood, the militancy of recent years becomes important. In the South, the dramatic struggles of a mass movement in the street have led to the registration of more than a million new black voters. In the ghettos of the North, where the enemies of Negro freedom are more subtle than Governor Wallace and the disintegrative power of poverty more compelling, there have been urban *Jacqueries,* spontaneous, unplanned riots, and the emergence among the ghetto young of a new pride of race. No one knows how deep these organizational efforts go (my impression is that the black militants have still to reach the majority of the black poor in any systematic fashion) and yet there is no doubt that there is more movement and thought and less despairing acceptance of social wrongs.

The Negroes are not alone in their insurgency. In California, some Mexican-Americans have organized economically in unions and exercised powerful political impact during the 1968 Democratic primary. In New York, Puerto Ricans have provided a mass base for unions in hospitals and public employment, and so have Negroes. Throughout the country, there are organizations of mothers on welfare demanding an end to the bureaucratic humiliations that are carefully structured into public assistance in America. And in Appalachia, poor whites have even had some limited success in the struggle against strip mining.

Yet, as I argued at some length in the book, *Toward a Democratic Left,* even if these rebellious movements grow in size and cohesion, even if they reach out to a majority of the poor, they will not be able to transform the society by themselves. Therefore the future of activism in the other America depends, in a considerable measure, upon what the non-poor do. This is certainly true if one thinks in terms of the need to create a vast majority coalition, for only such a movement would be capable of initiating the radical changes that are required if poverty is to be abolished in America. Paradoxically, the more fundamental and thoroughgoing an economic and social program, the more heterogeneous and inclusive must its supporters be. This is a truth not always appreciated by some of the sincerely self-righteous on the American Left. Even more immediately, insurgency among the poor is profoundly affected by the movement of the national economy. This fact leads to some larger generalizations about the dynamic of the other America in 1969.

When the Kennedy Administration began, the poor, with the exception of some Southern Negroes, were largely passive and pessimistic. This was partly a reflection of the daily life of the Eisenhower years: chronic unemployment and recession, official indifference, the invisibility of forty to fifty million people. The blacks made the first breakthrough below the Mason-Dixon line, and under the leadership of Martin Luther King, Jr., a general climate of hope developed. There was even the governmental policy of having the poor participate in the anti-poverty program. The economic and political upswing and the success of the black freedom movement in the South created the base for the beginning of a new spirit in the other America.

But, as that spirit expressed itself in various forms of militant protest, a new period began in 1965. The war in Vietnam began to dominate American domestic politics and the thirty billion dollars or more invested annually in that tragedy precluded any serious attempt at an "unconditional" war on poverty. The modest impact of the new economics was felt at the bottom of the American economy but in every way the tax cut was inversely—and perversely—related to need; the rich got the most benefit and profit, the poor the least. So the demands for change did not end. There was a great danger in this situation and it came to the fore in the Wallace campaign of 1968. When the struggle against poverty was part of a broad strategy of domestic economic expansion, white workers and members of the lower middle class had a certain common interest with blacks and the rest of the other America, even if they did not lose their prejudices. But when, because of Vietnam, the fight against want seemed to take on the aspect of a competition between the have-nots and the have-littles for scarce private and public goods, there were backlashers who feared that their own jobs, homes, and public places were being threatened.

At the beginning of 1969 it is uncertain what the next period will bring. In any case, I have no intention of indulging in prophecy. But it is not difficult to imagine how certain changes in government policy would affect the other America. If there is an economic downturn, the new activism of the poor —

those tentative essays in hope which we have seen —
will be turned into despair, most of it passive, some
of it dangerously angry. If the talk of "trading off" a
little unemployment in return for increased price stability becomes more than talk, and joblessness, as a
result, rises to five or six per cent, the extremely
modest employment gains of our recent efforts would
be abolished and the nation would return to the
status quo ante, or worse. Up to now, when the private sector has hired marginal workers, even with
federal inducements, it has done so only because a
relatively tight labor market had made it economically feasible to take a few — a very few — risks on
the hard-core jobless; the moment the official unemployment rate hits five per cent it will become economically imperative for corporations to fire those
men and women.

This would drastically affect the quality of life in
the other America. It would deprive the poor of part
of their already meager economic resources (the
richer a union, or a community organization, the
longer it can strike). It would confirm the suspicion,
which is never dispelled in the minds of the poor,
that the political order of the larger society is systematically rigged against those in it who are the
worst off. And most terrible of all, it would teach
those who had dared to be hopeful that America was
only kidding and that cynicism is the better part of
valor. Under such circumstances, a few would become even more militant; the many would sink back
into apathy.

Sometimes, when I contemplate this possibility, I
think the leaders of the United States have acted as
Trotsky said the German Communists did before the
rise of Hitler: they have infuriated all classes and
won none. The poor were given promises that were

not fulfilled, but the rhetoric made many workers and middle-class people fearful that they were being slighted, and the resulting political standoff alienated many of the most idealistic and active among the young. Politically, the entire society moved to the Right, and in the other America the fifth anniversary of the declaration of the war on poverty was a mockery.

The scenario need not be written this way. It is possible to make the massive planned social investments that would create the setting in which the poor would become more organized and determined to control their own political and economic destiny. But, as 1968 came to an end, the happy beginning was still not very imminent. It is not just that the statistical progress in abolishing poverty has been so modest or that the position of the "at risk" population of impoverished children and of blacks is so precarious and even explosive. It is more than that: there is a very real possibility that the spiritual gains of the poor — their new sense of dignity, their awareness that they need not forever be excluded from the democratic political process — are in danger. Looking back to the other America of 1962, it may be that in the years that have passed since then we have raised up the hopes of the most abused people of this land only in order to knock them down. ❧

Where Have All the Liberals Gone?

HARRY S. ASHMORE

Where have all the liberals gone? When the query was raised in these pages not long ago it seemed to me to carry with it a plaintive ring suitable for guitar accompaniment. This doubtless was a matter of context, since its author, Professor Joseph P. Lyford, lofted it from his office in Sproul Hall, on the besieged campus at Berkeley.

"The view of some faculty liberals," Lyford wrote, "that one should not get up-tight about the efforts of the super-militants because they have real grievances, brings back memories of the people who defended Senator Joseph McCarthy on the ground that he had the right objectives. The reflexive opposition of many liberals to the use of police on campus in any situation also brings back memories of the days when we applauded the dispatch of National Guardsmen to the University of Mississippi to protect James Meredith, and supported the occupation of Little Rock by soldiers sent there to make *Brown vs. Board of Education* a reality for a handful of Negro children."

The only issue I take with Professor Lyford is one of terminology. It is quite true that a great many who once stood on, or near, the high ground liberals profess to occupy have rushed off to join the battles that rack academe, or have fallen back before the onslaught. But the liberals, I think, are still there; weighing and balancing; distrusting the tug of their own emotions and the confused accounts of the campus actions; discounting the radical brand of revealed truth; displaying the quality that renders their breed conspicuous, and scorned, when passions run high — the capacity to entertain two opposing ideas at the same time.

In the case of the unrest at the universities, and of the larger issues from which it assertedly derives, this inner confrontation poses acceptance of a sweeping moral and intellectual indictment of the educational establishment. On the other hand, the charges in the case, which were drawn up by liberals, have been seized upon by self-proclaimed revolutionaries who claim the right to act as judge, jury, and executioner; who have displayed a marked incompetence to carry out any of these functions; and who have adopted a style of emotional coercion and physical violence that is patently anti-intellectual and, by liberal standards, at least amoral. This leaves liberals in the not unfamiliar position of being unable to defend either the attacker or the attacked.

This is perhaps inevitable, since the liberal, who understands contemporary events to be part of a continuum, is practically debarred from rhetorical interchange by the insistence of the black and the young that history has been repealed. In the excitement of declaring a radical disjuncture in the human progression, or of trying to create one, the busy revolutionaries concede no relevance to the finding of Russell Baker that "the discontent with modern American life had been widely sensed by the white middle class long before the campuses began to explode. The man in the gray flannel suit and the martini-drinking commuter on the 6:02 to Westchester had become symbols of middle-class self-contempt as early as the nineteen-fifties. The sense of the corporate game as a 'rat race' did not originate with today's campus rebels but with their fathers. Unhappiness with the proliferation of authoritarian bureaucracies armed with machinery for reducing individuality to coded numbers has been the theme of a hundred best-sellers since 1960."

Mr. Baker, the staff ironist of *The New York Times*, even went so far as to suggest that the rebels owe as much to the Right as to the Left. "In a sense, the student movement is the heir to the Goldwater movement. Both were born of rising middle-class discontent with what is called 'the quality of American life.' In some particulars, as on the war issue, the two were inimical. But on the central issue they were one: the modern superstate had ground down a man's freedom in the cause of perfecting its own organization; some better principle of organization had to be found."

It can be noted, too, that in their passion, their certitude, and their contempt for the law, the revolutionaries are one with the heirs of Goldwater, many of whom marched with George Wallace in the last Presidential contest. But the rhetoric is still that of the radical Left. It owes much of its tone and style to Marx even though the theoretical sense seems to have largely drained out. The liberal hears it as a familiar echo of his own past; being, by definition, over thirty, and of an intellectual bent, he is likely to bear scars from the ideological battles that raged in the academy throughout the Depression and the Cold War. No epithet can be attached to him he has not heard before; he is accustomed to appearing radical to conservatives, counter-revolutionary to radicals, and as a fink to activists of all persuasions.

When he permits himself the indulgence of self-pity the liberal recognizes that it is his fate to be praised, no less than condemned, for the wrong reasons. Thus John Cogley's summary of the current radical indictment accords him power and status he never had, holding that the post-industrial American society emergent in this generation is largely a liberal creation. In THE CENTER MAGAZINE Mr. Cogley observed that "liberalism, as its critics now see it, fulfilled none of its promises," and continued: "The record, they tell us, is shameful. The liberals were dominant in both political parties for thirty-five years or more. During the same years the black ghettos grew even more crowded, more impoverished, were cut off by an even greater gap than existed when the liberal effort began. During most of the same years the nation remained armed to the teeth and passed from one quasi-imperialist venture to another. The military-industrial complex fattened, the C.I.A.'s power reached out in all directions. The universities were corrupted by being intimately linked to the war system. One liberal program after another—the Peace Corps, the war on poverty, the Alliance for Progress —was begun with great hoopla and ended in disappointment. While the new suburbs grew richer and whiter, the cities became poorer and blacker. While the liberal rhetoric soared ever higher, the American situation kept growing more desperate."

The assumption here is that liberalism was an active political movement, or at least that its disciples sat in the places of power, or had effective access to those who did. A case, which I find less than overwhelming, can be made that this was the situation in the formative years of the New Deal. Franklin Roosevelt, faced with the collapse of the American economy, scrabbled around for whatever theory might promise quick repair and brought to Washington some of the theorists who had been demanding modification of laissez-faire government. But those who called themselves liberal never counted the late President one of their number, and before his long tenure was over he had amply proved them right.

The muddled and disjointed American welfare state was put together in the Roosevelt and Truman years, but as it came into being it represented not a triumph of liberal theory but an expedient departure from it. The new federal programs made obeisance to the humane social concerns of the liberal, and professed to preserve his cherished ideal of individual liberty, but in no case could they be considered a satisfactory compromise between these often conflicting goals.

This also was the era that produced the Cold War, and the enduring blight of the military-industrial complex that is its concomitant. If the liberals are to be blamed for this stultification of their ideals it must be for default. Divided in their own minds and loyalties by World War II and its aftermath, they were easily brushed aside by a rising managerial class that professed to have the ability to construct both weapons systems and foreign policy out of organization theory.

There was no President in the thirty-five-year stretch the liberals could call their own. Only one, John F. Kennedy, appeared to understand what they were talking about. The lone candidate who emerged from their ranks, Adlai Stevenson, warned of peril and asked hard questions, but he provided no real contest for the smiling Republican general who placed a bland, insensitive, reactive imprint on the central government. The placid Eisenhower style was greeted with relief after the clamorous Roosevelt-Truman years, but it quickly proved disastrous when circumstances forced Lyndon Johnson to speed up the tempo of the Washington apparatus. The liberal can argue that in the whole generational span the issues he considered most urgent were misinterpreted when they were not ignored.

This has continued to be the case with Richard Nixon's Administration, which seems to locate his predecessor's failures primarily in public relations and merchandising. But it is no less true of the radical movement, which, as Professor Lyford noted, also has adapted to the histrionic demands of television, and played a symbolic game until the ratings dropped and the angry young men could attract attention only by crossing the threshold of physical violence. The justification for this, or for the coercion by emotional blackmail which the threat of violence makes possible, is all-embracing. In the apocalyptic view of those who identify themselves with the red flag, the black flag, or the hippies' wilted flower, the corruption of the American middle-class society (culture is the vogue word) has long since passed beyond hope of redemption. Logic, then, as well as morality, requires that the convert help pull down the tottering structure or, if he can't stand the sight of blood, at least withdraw while it collapses of its own rotten weight. To try to patch up the society by reform is not merely futile but cowardly and dishonorable.

John Seeley, characteristically, has put the proposition more gently, but he also broadens its scope well beyond the barricades. Intellectuals, he and Professor Alvin W. Gouldner wrote in a call for a radical sociological caucus, should not confine their "activism to melioristic efforts 'within the system.' We feel," they said, "that this is a time when efforts to develop clear alternatives to the present often require that we work 'outside' the system. For we believe that efforts to solve contemporary problems will be crippled unless they can adopt a critical stance toward complacent liberalism. Indeed, it seems to us the repressive side of conventional liberalism was made fully public in the mutual accommodation between Vice-President Hubert Humphrey and Mayor Richard Daley at the Chicago Convention of the Democratic Party."

The key word here is "repressive." In its current over-usage the term covers everything from the unrestrained use of nightsticks by ham-handed cops to the requirement that college students receive grades. To the more advanced therapeutic school the process of repression, undertaken in order to condition the young to the service of a repressive society, starts with diaper-training. A raised voice, or even an eyebrow, can be seen as repressive; the intent of the raiser is of no account, only the psychic damage done by the received impression. Since repression is declared indefensible, any means of resisting or countering it is justified. True violence, in the litany of the S.D.S., lies in the society, and he who counters with violence is a liberator.

This is the point of separation between liberals and radicals. Not finding the apocalyptic view supported by his own experience and historical concepts, the liberal cannot accept the logic that justifies the means the putative revolution must employ if it is to move toward its professed ends. Moreover, he is unable to identify the ends with any precision, since they cannot be articulated but apparently are largely *felt* by those in the vanguard. At the head of the long list of matters declared irrelevant by the revolutionaries is one the liberal considers the prior question: What happens after the revolution has effected a radical transfer of power? At this point the liberal begins to run out of questions altogether, for he finds himself being led into theological territory, and he is neither equipped nor disposed to deal with matters of faith.

ॐ

Still, the revolution has an undeniable attraction. "It is unfair to blame the students for not being able to see the big issues," Russell Baker has written. "At least they try, which is more than can be said for much of the discontented middle class. On a few things, like the war and the race issue, they have succeeded." The blacks, who have their own sometimes parallel movement going in full cry, have a very clear idea of what the big issues are in their special situation. Negroes are seeking power in order to satisfy the traditional demands of a genuinely oppressed and generally disadvantaged minority. In either case there is a powerful plucking at the conscience of the liberal, who tries to steer his own course between the poles of individual liberty and social justice.

Encyclopaedia Britannica defines liberalism as "the creed, philosophy, and movement which is committed to freedom as a method and policy in government, as an organizing principle in society, and as a way of life for the individual and community." So it was, in its seventeenth-century beginnings, in its eighteenth-century revolutionary triumphs, and in its nineteenth-century consolidation as the dominant political order of the West. But by the turn of our own century it was clear that Adam Smith's invisible hand, which was presumed to set human affairs aright if all were guaranteed freedom of thought and economic action, had disappeared in the smoke of the urbanizing Industrial Revolution. In an increasingly complex society free men could starve, and properly endowed democrats could founder in political impotence. In 1911 one of the high priests of the order, L. T. Hobhouse, of Oxford, wrote: "Liberty without equality is a name of noble sound and squalid meaning." Summarizing the condition of liberalism in the second half of the twentieth century, Britannica notes: "It might certainly be said that the classical and largely negative phases of liberalism had gone with the winds of history. What was not clear was whether this applied also to the democratic and welfare phases of the affirmative liberal state."

The surviving liberalism can best be described as a cast of mind and a code of personal conduct. The commitment is to the maintenance of an open society which accords all its members social justice. The liberal recognizes that, in his own time at least, the ideal is impossible to attain, and that his primary task may be to see that the necessary compromises are not fatal. While his own history has made him skeptical of the short-range results of democracy, he sees no substitute for self-government as the only feasible check on the managerial and scientific/technological elites required for the functioning of an advanced society. He acknowledges the existence of power, and distrusts it; he accepts the use of force only when it is allied with constituted authority and the rule of law; he puts his ultimate trust in the capacity of men to reconcile their differences without coercion if society can be made to approximate Thomas Jefferson's free marketplace of ideas. There can be no community without consensus, he holds, and an enduring consensus can only grow out of dialogue. Hence tolerance is the liberal's cardinal virtue, and he cherishes civility as the literal and essential derivation of civilization.

The stance, of course, is not satisfactory to moralists. In his concern with the parts of society, and his acceptance of imperfection, the liberal offends classical philosophers, who condemn him as a pragmatist addicted to an untidy pluralism. Holding that if there is ever to be a new man he will be no less the product of evolution than the current model, he cuts himself off from the radical utopians. The vision of the apocalypse is alien to the liberal not only because of the gratuitous cruelty of its mass indictment but because he can find no rational basis for locating all of mankind's moral guilt among those who do not profess the innocence of self-alienation. He would agree with Stringfellow Barr that "it's very hard to think when you are top dog," but he would insist that coherent thought is hardly easier for the underdog, beset as he is by real and fancied persecutions and the debilitating necessities of survival. Thinking, in his view, requires a degree of detachment, of self-doubt, even of self-irony, all of which are conspicuous elements in the liberal style and are conspicuously absent in that of the radical.

The liberal's habit of skepticism, and his concession that his own human limitations embody the possibility of error, apply even in the most weighty considerations of life and death. Thus in the great days of religious influence, and now in its period of decline, he might find himself inside the institutional church criticizing its professions and practices, or outside attacking the whole system of theological thought. In either position he respects the other. Conceding that he was incapable of sharing the moment of truth of a Tolstoy or a Simone Weil, Sir Herbert

Read wrote: "To those who have not received it, the grace of God seems an arbitrary gift, and I resent the suggestion of the initiates that we who live in outer darkness do so because of our intellectual pride. I am completely humble in my attitude toward the mystery of life, and accept gratefully such intuitions as come to me from the writings of the mystics, and from works of art."

The liberal is properly accused of having difficulty in deciding what to do in the face of crisis. However, he knows what not to do — what, indeed, he cannot do without abandoning the values he lives by. When Marxist theory emerged in the last century to challenge the economic and social precepts of Western liberal democracy, he could find merit in its scathing analysis and in some of its prescriptions. He could become a socialist, and many liberals did. But he could not become a Communist, or at least could not remain one after he faced up to the inhuman physical and spiritual repressions the Marxist revolution would require on the road to utopia. Irving Howe, in a more or less autobiographical essay in *Commentary*, has recounted the shattering experience of the group of influential New York intellectuals who lived through the unmasking of Joseph Stalin: "During the nineteen-thirties and -forties their radicalism was anxious, problematic, and beginning to decay at the very moment it was adopted. They had no choice: the crisis of socialism was worldwide, profound, with no end in sight, and the only way to avoid that crisis was to bury oneself, as a few did, in the left-wing sects. Some of the New York writers had gone through the 'political school' of Stalinism, a training in coarseness from which not all recovered; some even spent a short time in the organizational coils of the Communist Party . . . [but]

no version of orthodox Marxism could retain a hold on intellectuals who had gone through the trauma of abandoning the Leninist *Weltanschauung* and had experienced the depth to which the politics of this century, most notably the rise of totalitarianism, called into question the once-sacred Marxist categories. From now on, the comforts of the system would have to be relinquished."

In what Seymour Krim has described as "the over-cerebral, Europeanish, sterilely citified, pretentiously alienated" world of New York's radical intellectuals, where endless polemics provide much of the mental exercise, the old anguish of the nineteen-thirties has continued, in one way or another, down to the present day. Here is Professor Howe's reflection on the inevitable aftermath of the great Stalinist cleavage: "Like anti-capitalism, anti-Communism was a tricky politics, all too open to easy distortion. Like anti-capitalism, anti-Communism could be put to the service of ideological racketeering and reaction. Just as ideologues of the fanatic Right insisted that by some ineluctable logic anti-capitalism led to a Stalinist terror, so ideologues of the authoritarian Left, commandeering the same logic, declared that anti-Communism led to the politics of Dulles and Rusk. There is, of course, no 'anti-capitalism' or 'anti-Communism' in the abstract; these take on political flesh only when linked with a larger body of programs and values, so that it becomes clear what *kind* of 'anti-capitalism' or 'anti-Communism' we are dealing with."

To young revolutionaries who consider all history ancient, the foregoing is also consigned to the wonderfully capacious category of irrelevance. Yet two of the most durable gurus of the movement, the two who have earned acceptance across the age barrier by attempting to endow the revolution with some coherent theoretical structure, are conspicuous products of the period. Professor Howe places Paul Goodman in the political spectrum by describing him as "a very courageous writer, who stuck to his anarchist beliefs through years in which he was mocked and all but excluded from the New York journals." The elusive doctrine of Herbert Marcuse, he finds, is based on "contempt for tolerance on the ground that it is a veil for subjection, a rationale for maintaining the status quo, and his consequent readiness to suppress 'regressive' elements in the population lest they impede social 'liberation.' About these theories, which succeed in salvaging the worst of Leninism, Henry David Aiken has neatly remarked: 'Whether garden-variety liberties can survive the ministrations of such "liberating tolerance" is not a question that greatly interests Marcuse.' "

The question does, of course, greatly interest liberals, who find the most striking contradiction of the new movement in its nihilistic devotion to the personal desires of its members and its calculated dismissal of the rights of others. If for no other reason, the legitimacy of the revolution would be questioned by conventional Marxists because of its rejection of the stern, puritan self-discipline the master demanded of all his followers, high and low. If even the mild dissidence of the Czechs proved anathema to the mellowing Soviet commissars, it is easy to imagine what would happen to a cadre of pot-smoking, free-loving, gut-communicating rebels in Mao's China, where the real, 100-proof doctrine is still in vogue.

It is evident that Marx, and all the other radical philosophers who approached their analytic and dialectic task with the tools of scholarship and the standards of science, have given way to Freud as the godhead of liberation. A new sensibility has been proclaimed, in which the rational, insofar as it is admitted at all, is subordinate to the sensory. Professor Howe describes its basis as the psychology of unobstructed need: "Men should satisfy those needs which are theirs, organic to their bodies and psyches, and to do this they now must learn to discard or destroy all those obstructions, mostly the result of cultural neurosis, which keep them from satisfying their needs. This does not mean that the moral life is denied; it only means that in the moral economy costs need not be entered as a significant item. In the current vocabulary, it becomes a matter of everyone doing 'his own thing,' and once all of us are allowed to do 'his own thing' a prospect of easing harmony unfolds. Sexuality is the ground of being, and vital sexuality the assurance of the moral life."

It follows that the manifestation of the revolution must be consciously irrational and profoundly anti-intellectual. Viewing it from without, it also appears in its public aspect to be uncompromisingly self-centered, trivial, and, if one can be pardoned the expression, irrelevant to the purposes of what professes to be, among other things, a cult of love. The dully repetitive obscenity of the early days has developed into an exhibitionist sexuality that causes the uninitiate to wonder whether it is not, in fact, a substitute for the real thing.

As we grope for the inner meaning of the movement we are warned by an insider, Susan Sontag, that it must be viewed as a broadly cultural rather than a narrowly political phenomenon. "Our task is seen as not one of forming but of *dismantling* a consciousness," Miss Sontag wrote in *Ramparts*, "becoming simpler, discharging dead weight. Hence the anti-intellectualism of the brightest kids; their distrust of books, school; their attraction to non-verbalizable experiences like rock and to states, such as that under drugs, which confound verbalizing; their belief in instinct, in vibrations."

❦

The liberal devotion to analysis, speculation, and rational judgment is clearly ruled out as inimical to sensuousness, the major component of the new sensibility. It would seem, then, that if any scholarly investigator is qualified to make his way across this formidable barrier it would be a sympathetic dramatist, whose profession involves him in the interpretation and projection of emotion. However, it has been recorded in the most literate repository of radical writ, *The New York Review of Books,* that in a limited but not insignificant engagement on the cultural revolutionary front, the dean of the Yale Drama School, Robert Brustein, came out a shaken and chastened man.

Dean Brustein had established his radical credentials by praising what he called the Third Theatre, the off-off-Broadway drama epitomized by *America Hurrah, Dynamite Tonight,* and *MacBird!,* which he continues to defend as works of genuine imagination and originality. It then became his duty to welcome the Living Theatre to New Haven, even though he had already recognized the touring company of young American performers as "inflamed with a sense of mission that was less theatrical or even political than religious and evangelical."

In the course of its engagement at Yale, which ended with a police bust, Dean Brustein found that the company's invitation to the audience to participate in free theater quickly expired in the case of any who arose to question the antic action. When a female student launched into a denunciation of the Living Theatre she was promptly "hustled offstage by a group of performers who embraced her into silence — unbuttoning her blouse, feeling her legs, and shutting her mouth with kisses." Thus, in the name of freedom, the extemporaneous drama was summarily reduced to an exercise in constraint and control. "The company, particularly vulnerable to ridicule because of its lack of humor, allowed no alien laughter ever to penetrate its relentless solemnity, self-righteousness, and self-importance."

Having made his attack in the pages of *The New York Review*, where it was certain to arouse the radical community, Dean Brustein felt constrained to accept a subsequent invitation to participate in a symposium entitled "Theatre or Therapy" which paired him off with the leaders of the Living Theatre company, Julian Beck and Judith Malina. The New York division of the New Left establishment was well represented. Nat Hentoff served as moderator, Paul Goodman was one of the discussants, and Norman Mailer was in the highly vocal audience.

The symposium was scheduled in an austere former Friends' Meeting House near Gramercy Park where audience and participants were arranged in pews in a stark white auditorium. To Dean Brustein's dramatist's eye it seemed a splendid setting for rational discourse. He presented a sample of what actually followed in the *Review*:

" ' "Theatre or Therapy" is a rather loaded topic title,' I said, 'but it does begin to indicate the kind of controversy that is occupying the theater today where the central question seems to be: To what extent should a production be oriented toward the audience, to what extent toward the actors, and to what extent toward the playwright? One's answer to this is affected by one's attitude toward some important issues of our time: freedom versus responsibility, activist theater versus non-activist theater, free improvisation versus disciplined skill, process versus presentation, and so forth.'

"A voice from the balcony: 'What the hell is disciplined skill?'

"A voice from the orchestra: 'Shut up, you twerp.'

"From the balcony: 'Fuck you, I'm asking him a question.'

"From the orchestra: 'We'll listen to you later. He's doing the talking now.'

" 'My own position quite simply stated is this,' I continued. 'I believe the theater to be served best when it is served by supremely gifted individuals possessed of superior vision and the capacity to express this in enduring form. In short, I believe in the theater as a place of high art.'

"The heckler: 'We're all supremely gifted individuals.'

"Brustein: 'I doubt that very much.'

"The heckler: 'Up against the wall.' "

The symposium continued in this vein until the predictable dissolution by bedlam. When Dean Brustein cited Chekhov as an example of a gifted individual, the voice from the balcony dismissed the playwright with the usual epithet; before the evening was over the same judgment had been rendered on Ibsen, Shakespeare, and Euripides, and, in summary, on "all fucking liberal intellectuals and their fucking discussions." Paul Goodman fared no better even though he praised the Living Theatre and went on to discuss the cherished hippie analogy between contemporary unrest and the Protestant Reformation.

" 'Don't think you're like the Christians in the catacombs,' he said. 'You're not going to destroy the institutions, you're going to reform them. You talk like there's a cataclysm coming, but there isn't. ... The institutions will survive. ...'

" 'No, they won't,' shouted Rufus Collins, a black member of the company who had suddenly materialized on the floor of the hall. 'Because we're going to destroy them.'

" 'You're not going to destroy them,' replied Goodman, good-humoredly. 'You can't destroy them. And you won't even reform them unless you can think up some ideas. I've lived through movements like this before, and I'm always struck by the poverty of ideas. In two thousand years, there hasn't been a single new revolutionary idea.'

" 'We'll destroy them,' Collins screamed. 'We'll create a cataclysm.'

" 'You're not powerful enough. You're just an idiosyncratic fringe group like the Anabaptists. You don't have the capacity even to close down the universities.'

" 'Close them down, close them down,' Collins shouted. 'Fuck the universities!'

" 'If you start to do that,' Goodman said, still maintaining his sweet reasonableness, 'they'll just put you on a reservation somewhere and keep you quiet.'

" 'They're going to put us on reservations and kill us,' Collins said, his voice now cracking with fury. 'They're going to exterminate us, just like the Indians — the racists, the genocides. They're going to kill all of us.'

" 'No, they won't,' Goodman answered. 'They'll just feed you some LSD and keep you pacified.'

"Norman Mailer chose to make his entrance at this point, lumbering down the aisle to his seat just as Goodman was replying to one of Rufus Collins' assaults on America's machine culture.

" 'Don't blame everything on technology,' Goodman said. 'It's too easy. Just the other day, I listened to a young fellow sing a very passionate song about how technology is killing us and all that. . . . But before he started, he bent down and plugged his electric guitar into the wall socket.'

"Collins began jumping up and down in fury. 'That boy has thrown away his guitar. He's taken off his clothes. He's going up to the mountains where he's using only his voice and his feet. Fuck technology!'

" 'Why are you wearing glasses then?' asked a man sitting nearby.

" 'Because I can't see,' Collins screamed. 'Fuck technology. Fuck technology.'

"Mailer applauded loudly and conspicuously. Goodman shrugged and sat down on the floor in front of his seat with his back to the audience. . . . "

I have excerpted Dean Brustein's account at length because it seems to me to typify a convergence of the dominant strains in the current radical movement: casual brutality and calculated chaos offered as ends in themselves, and justified as the means toward a liberating group therapy. "The first night we did *Paradise Now* at Yale — the night we got busted," Judith Malina said, "we all came out of the theater on each other's shoulders and into the streets. It was a very beautiful and joyous moment, everybody was feeling like something beautiful was happening." The moment of truth and beauty was hardly shared by the semi-raped critic with the unbuttoned blouse, and certainly not by Dean Brustein, who earlier had written of the same performance: "The most depressing thing of all was how easily university students, and even some of their teachers, responded to the baldest of slogans, and the most simplistic interpretations of reality. . . . Love and brotherhood were continually on the lips of the actors, but no actors in my experience have bristled with so much aggression or more successfully galvanized the aggression of the spectator. . . . It was, finally, not a vision of human freedom that one took away from *Paradise Now,* but vague, disturbing memories of the youth rallies in Hitler's Nuremberg."

Bruno Bettelheim, the University of Chicago psychologist, made this analysis of the individual conduct of student rebels: "My own observations of leaders of the radical Left whom I got to know well are that in most cases their intellectual abilities were developed very highly at much too early an age, at the expense of their emotional development. Though very bright, some of them remain emotionally fixated at the age of the temper tantrum. . . . Psychologically, I found most student extremists hating themselves as intensely as they hate the Establishment — a self-hatred they try to escape from by fighting *any* establishment."

If there is substance in this view, the youth movement is not, and cannot be, a revolution, and for all the disruption it has occasioned, there is good reason to reject its partisans' claim that it is at least a manifestation of the pre-revolutionary stage of a declining society. Dean Brustein contends that the New Left is now visibly turning in upon itself. The fact that the students' quasi-revolutionary gestures are "aimed not against the Pentagon or the napalm-producing factories, but rather against the university itself (for all its faults, still one of the last outposts of civilization and humane values), only indicates that the desire for effectiveness *somewhere* far transcends the desire for effective change."

This may be taken as a dim view from the Right, or from above, but the movement lately has come under even more stringent criticism from the Left. In the radical *Guardian* Eugene Genovese wrote: "The mindless anarchism of wild-in-the-streets having ended in the bankruptcy every politically knowledgeable man predicted for it, the New Left has turned to a new and fake Leninism. Flower power, non-violence, love everybody, Quaker radicalism, and participatory democracy have finally emerged in discernible colors: a cult of violence, a marked totalitarian temperament, and a thoroughgoing contempt for the claims of individual freedom. . . . Notwithstanding its heroic efforts and genuine accomplishments, the movement early betrayed a bourgeois elitism, disguised as egalitarianism; a contempt for historical experience, disguised as existentialist philosophy; and, above all, a passion for the destruction of any system of rational order, disguised as a demand for total participation. That the present fad (and it is only a fad) is 'Maoist,' rather than something else, ought not to surprise us either, for the so-called cultural revolution in China has assumed the aspect of a nihilist's heaven."

The overt violence on the campuses, then, may well mark the beginning of the end of what probably will be recorded as more localized aberration than mass movement. As of now, however, the situation is patently intolerable, as the scenarists, if not the bemused bit players, always intended it to be. So, with the usual American proclivity for acting after the fact, the middle-class society apparently is nearing the end of what has seemed to me to be a remarkable, unprecedented permissiveness. Now there is a threat of genuine repression to replace the loudly denounced psychological brand, which can be seen in retrospect as not much more than an expression of disapproval by consenting elders intimidated by their own offspring.

This, I suspect, is where the liberals come in. If they could not embrace the putative revolution because of its mindless cruelty, they also are bound to reject the self-righteous and punitive counteractions proposed in the name of law and order. One can no more impute to the Senate's chief inquisitor, John McClellan, of Arkansas, an abiding concern for restoring the intellectual values of the academy than one could expect to find in the late Joseph McCarthy a devotion to the Bill of Rights.

It is, of course, necessary to put an end to assault and arson, but cooling off the student bodies is the least part of the problem. It will not be done in any case by the grandstanding of such as Lyndon Johnson's pet philosopher, Eric Hoffer, who was an inevitable premier witness before the McClellan Committee cameras. All the colleges need, Hoffer proclaimed, is tough administrators who "will spit on their hands and say, 'Who do I kill today?' "

On the day Mr. Hoffer made this considerable contribution to reënforcing the rebel cause, Jacques Barzun came down from the ruins of Columbia to recite before a House Committee a list of the educational establishment's chronic ailments that go back to the days when campus intellectuals were fretting about the complacency and conformity of the "silent generation." It all began, as Professor Barzun said, when the demands of World War II greatly expanded the public-service role of the university: "Inevitable in time of war, this enlargement continued after 1945. It turned the university into a catch-all institution, ready to do what government, industry, foundations, and private donors wanted.

With the best intentions, faculty members became globetrotters and project directors. . . . The university's true service to society was obscured and damaged by these new and multiplying services; teaching was neglected; buzzing activity replaced quiet thought. . . . The university became a common target, an object of complaint, pressure, and demand. By its nature, it could not fight back. It was vulnerable and it fell."

The liberal has an inevitable concern with this institutional collapse. The fallen university is his spiritual and often his actual home. As Professor Barzun said, if the university is to be restored it will have to be endowed once again with the traditional liberal values, "the way of discussion, civility, and decent behavior." The monumental task is possible only to those who spurn the punitive, reject the conspiracy theory of history, and understand that nobody is guilty because everybody is. And certainly restoration will demand full exercise of the liberal habit scorned by radicals as an outmoded manifestation of the Protestant ethic: hard, concentrated, self-sacrificing work.

The liberal also may be indispensable to melioration of the black man's agony in his transition into the larger white society. In any case he can't escape involvement, since this is the final stage of the task liberals set for themselves in the earliest days of Abolition, when they insisted that slavery must end not as a matter of charity but of human right. Termination of chattel ownership of one man by another may be the only enduring triumph humanists can claim in the entire sweep of recorded history, and its full promise will not be fulfilled as long as the American society excludes any man on the basis of race or color.

The long political and legal struggle for institutional desegregation has advanced in this generation to the point where it is becoming possible to get on with the even more difficult job of social integration. For all the reasons he could not support the youth revolution, the liberal is bound to reject as expedient and destructive the demand that the terminal effort be abandoned in favor of a return to segregation in the name of Black Power and racial therapy. He stands on Harry Golden's premise: "To say that the Negroes cannot catch up is to use the results of racial segregation as a means to perpetuate it."

If the shouting ever dies down, the brief list of liberal verities may again become comprehensible to the young and the black, and perhaps even to the middle class as it swings between complacency and panic. The lessons to be drawn from the raucous action and reaction of the nineteen-sixties seem to me to confirm the traditional liberal view that innocence arbitrarily prolonged is ignorance; entry into the world of ideas requires apprenticeship; the senses are important but not ultimate; feeling is a part of learning but only an auxiliary to wisdom; the past is prelude and no man can move forward without first looking back.

In this perspective it is possible to see that, while anger and frustration come easily to the young, so should laughter, the healthy, gay, unashamed laughter that can cure a sick society when it once again sounds on campus to mark the pleasures of discovery. When they can laugh again the young will observe that in the receding ranks of their elders fools are far more numerous than scoundrels, and they may be comforted to find that even a fool is capable of loving his children. ෯

Why Students Revolt

STRINGFELLOW BARR

Could the diagnosis run as follows? Universities have hitherto been run by a profession. In western Europe and its cultural offspring, the Colonies, this profession had once been the clergy, but was now the academic scholars. Throughout most of its history, the academic profession afforded its members leisure for learning and teaching but only a very modest salary. Academics were assumed to respect learning more than wealth, just as priests and ministers placed service to God and to the community above wealth; just as doctors placed healing the sick above making money; and just as lawyers were expected to place justice in the courts above their fee. Whenever priests or academics, doctors or lawyers, have ceased thinking of their fees or salaries as designed merely to free them to follow their learned profession and have thought of themselves as selling their knowledge or art to the highest bidder, men have denounced them as corrupt. Corrupt churchmen, or academics, or lawyers, or physicians have been denounced as traitors to their professions when they did what countless merchants and businessmen did without blushing: made as much money as possible. Does this mean that when a society's learned professionals act like businessmen they corrupt their society and it becomes a "sick" society?

A relatively recent document on this sort of corruption was the account of the American Medical Association's fight against a federal system of medical insurance that Richard Harris published a year or two ago in *The New Yorker*. But long before that, Julien Benda exposed the corruption of intellectuals in general in his book, *La Trahison des Clercs*. Within the past few months several books on the American university have exhibited the same corruption. One of them, *The Closed Corporation* (Random House), by James Ridgeway, is a conscious exposé. Another, *The Academic Revolution* (Doubleday), by David Riesman and Christopher Jencks, celebrates the triumph of the professor-entrepreneur but, in doing so, lets us see the same shift of purpose from intellectual struggle to worldly success. Jacques Barzun's newest book, *The American University* (Harper & Row), is a more sophisticated account of academe, but he, too, illuminates the corruption.

It is, at least in part, against this corruption that the students of every continent are now in revolt. There is little evidence that they know what a university's true function is. Why should they? But they quite rightly reject what Mr. Ridgeway pictures as the military-industrial-*academic* complex. If we oldsters wonder why today's students are so unlike what we were when we were students, we might remember how little the universities of America are like those which we attended. For, indeed, the money-changers are in the temple, the temple of learning. Although the general public, for the most part, does not know it, the university professor has turned go-getter. His booty includes a fat salary from a business firm, eager to wear that professional look, or a juicy fee as consultant, or a federal grant big enough to suport him and a staff of assistants. In this last case, our professor is in a position to squeeze the president for promotions and other favors by threatening to move himself and his staff to some other campus. In this atmosphere of increasing affluence, of classified information, and of pleasant expense accounts, the professor too often teaches as little as possible or not at all.

Faced with this massive corruption of what was once the purpose of a profession, the student joins the revolt against The Establishment. He is as outraged as any zealot of the Reformation period faced with the massive corruption of the Church. Can he really be blamed? He was used to the lying television commercial, but he had thought of the university as a community concerned, not with power, not with force, not with fraud, but with discovering the truth and proclaiming it. The university, as anxious to restore its "image" as any other corporation, cannot appease its students by branding them as lazy, pot-smoking, self-indulgent hypocrites, themselves as corrupt as any seat of higher learning could possibly be. The issue is not whether the incoming freshman class is, or is not, less normal than the faculty. It used to be assumed that the faculty knew of some better things than money and power to live by. It is true that by the fifties "useful" courses had almost completely replaced the traditional liberal arts — the arts of reading, writing, speaking, listening, whether the symbols were those of a poem or a mathematical proof. With courses that were safe, sound, and thought to be practical, one might hope to end up the vice-president of a business corporation and to own a home in the suburbs.

Then, in 1956, William H. Whyte in *The Organization Man* made a mockery of this vice-presidential suburban dream. It was widely used in undergraduate courses in sociology. Madison Avenue had taught the American people to stop speaking critically of private enterprise and to call it admiringly "free enterprise." Today business executives, along with all other Very Important Persons, are denounced as The Establishment. The young sneer at the C.I.A., the F.B.I., and General Hershey. They do not feel disgraced by jail. As sons of that Man in the Gray Flannel Suit, they are prepared to go barefoot, unshaven and unshorn, and to burn not only their draft cards but a flag or two. Many of them believe that the political process is as rotten as the rigged price system and that it should not be reformed but sabotaged. Hence riots and guerrilla tactics in the cities, and sufficient noise to drown out candidates at the hustings.

In the long run, calling the police cannot save the universities. ২৬

The Reluctant Death of Sovereignty

ARNOLD J. TOYNBEE

The claim to sovereignty is a claim made by the members of a community of whatever scale to be at liberty, not only de facto but de jure, and morally too, to assert their collective will against the wills of all outsiders. The outsiders, however, also have a word to say about this; and, up to the present moment in history, every self-styled sovereign community has had to reckon with the independent collective wills of other communities with which it has been coexisting. Thus, a community's claim to sovereignty is countered by rival claims to the same license; and, so far, this limitation of sovereignty has been universal, because, up to now, even the most extensive of the empires that have risen and fallen have stopped far short of embracing the entire human race. This means that there has never been a community completely sovereign de facto.

In the modern world before the Second World War, the number of communities that claimed to be sovereign was between sixty and seventy. Within the past twenty-three years the number has almost doubled and still threatens to increase. The people of each of the former subject territories that were tied together in the pre-war West European colonial empires have claimed separate sovereignty for themselves, and some of these local successor-states of the disbanded colonial empires seem to be dissolving in their turn into still smaller sovereign fragments.

The increasing political fragmentation of the human race is a paradox in an age in which technology is "annihilating distance"; and the paradox is also a menace, for the "annihilation of distance" opens the way for either fruitful cooperation or disastrous collision. A politically wide-awake minority of the human race has been aware of this menace since the invention of atomic weapons. The problem is to awaken the majority, who are still taking national sovereignty for granted as one of the facts of life and — more than that — as a basic human right, indeed as the supreme political objective for any community that has not yet attained it, however incapable the community may be of exercising sovereignty effectively.

This present world-wide cult of national sovereignty is strange, considering that the concept originated in one part only of the human race — the Western part — and that, even there, did not become prevalent until a fairly recent stage of Western history. The first dramatically successful assertion of it in the West was that of the King of France, Philip IV, against the Papacy, represented by Pope Boniface VIII, at the end of the thirteenth century. Between that date and the end of the first World War in 1918, Western society reorganized itself progressively into a set of sovereign states. The final step along the road was the break-up of the supra-national Danubian Habsburg monarchy into a cluster of separate sovereign national successor-states. Since then, the political reorganization of mankind into sovereign communities has spread beyond the bounds of the Western society until it has become virtually world-wide.

This triumphal progress of the concept of national sovereignty over a period of five and a half centuries is impressive. It is proof of the concept's potency in captivating human hearts and winning their enthusiastic allegiance. The cult has become mankind's major religion, a religion whose god is a Moloch to whom parents are willing to make human sacrifices of their sons and of themselves and of all their fellow human beings too, if a "conventional" war should escalate into a nuclear one.

States of all kinds have usually been deified by a majority of their subjects. The Christians' exceptional refusal to worship the Roman Empire got them into trouble with the Roman Imperial Government. The Christians were surely in the right both on the question of fact and on the question of morals. States may appear godlike on account of their formidable power over human beings, but this power is not really divine; it is merely collective human power, and there are limits to its dominion over individual human beings. An individual can defeat the power of a state if he is willing to suffer martyrdom; and there are occasions on which martyrdom is a moral duty, for the governments of states, being human, are as prone as any other human beings to commit crimes and sins that ought not to be condoned by their subjects. Far from being divine, states are nothing but man-made public utilities. They are as unsuitable as gas-works and water-works for being made into objects of worship and into focuses of emotion.

The peculiar, and peculiarly dangerous, feature of the worship of modern national states is that this has been keyed up to an unusually high emotional pitch by a special charge of post-Christian fanaticism. There has always been a streak of fanaticism in Christianity; and when the Western peoples became progressively disillusioned with the Western Christian Church, in reaction to a series of ecclesiastical scandals culminating in the Catholic-Protestant wars of religion, the fanaticism for which Christianity had previously provided a vent was left, for a time, without an alternative outlet.

This low point in the temperature chart of Western

fanaticism was, in a negative respect at any rate, the halcyon age of Western history. The breathing-space was, however, brief. It did not begin until after the revocation of the Edict of Nantes (a revocation that was the last major Western exhibition of Christian fanaticism), and it came to an end at the outbreak of the American Revolutionary War. The respite was, in fact, approximately coincident with the lifetime of Voltaire; and, though Voltaire was long-lived, even the longest human life is short in terms of the time-scale of history. This period of less than a century was a golden age for an enlightened minority of Westerners, but it left the majority restless and uneasy. During this short interlude, the fanaticism of this majority was pent up, and it looked about to find a new outlet.

Eighteenth-century Western man was, in fact, the man in the parable who has cast out one devil and finds that he cannot abide living in a swept and garnished house that has no diabolical tenant. Accordingly, when the unhappy man finds seven devils more wicked than the first, he eagerly invites them in; and the new devils he adopts are the post-Christian national states. In present-day psychological terms, the libido that Western man had withdrawn from Christianity before the close of the seventeenth century was decanted by him, before the close of the eighteenth century, into nationalism. Modern nationalism is the ancient idolatrous worship of collective human power raised to an unprecedented degree of intensity by the infusion into it of post-Christian fanaticism.

The intensity of worship of the idol of the national state is, of course, no evidence that national sovereignty provides a satisfactory basis for the political organization of mankind in the atomic age. The truth is the very opposite. While our hearts are still blindly devoted to national sovereignty, our heads are already telling us that in this age national sovereignty spells mass suicide. The supreme political question of our time is whether the head is going to persuade the heart. Will allegiance to the fatal ideal of national sovereignty bĕ transferred to the ideal of world government in time to save mankind from self-destruction?

It will require a break with a cherished political habit. Human nature shrinks from even minor changes of habit, because the changing of habits is always unpleasant and is sometimes positively painful. Yet even this may be a much lesser evil than the penalty entailed in clinging to a habit that has become lethal. We have either to break with it or to destroy ourselves. If we now decide that we must jettison the institution of national sovereignty, we need not fear that we shall lose ourselves in a political vacuum.

There is a practical alternative to nationalism in ecumenism. The evidence for the practicality of both these forms of political organization is the same. World-states have played as prominent a part in human history, so far, as fractional states have. Of course, no would-be world-state has yet been literally world-wide. Only within the last 150 years has the progress of technology made a literally world-wide world-state technically possible. Today we possess the technological and organizational know-how for administering human affairs on a world-wide scale. Indeed, on the economic plane, in contrast to the political, there are already a number of private business concerns which operate on a scale that extends to the whole habitable and traversable surface of our planet. We could organize our political life, too, on this scale at any moment if we only had the will to do so.

Our predecessors, equipped with only muscle-power applied to overland traction and with only wind-power applied to seafaring, succeeded in uniting politically, and in holding together for centuries on end, territories and populations larger than those of even the largest present-day national states. By our standards, the equipment of these past empire-builders was rudimentary. They surmounted their technological handicaps because they had the will. If we had the same will, our present technological equipment would enable us to construct, with ease, a world-state of literally world-wide dimensions.

ॐ

The political history of the West, the region in which the concept of national sovereignty arose about five and a half centuries ago, is illuminating and, on the whole, encouraging. The background to this history is the rise and fall of the Roman Empire.

The rise of the Roman Empire gave an eleventh-hour reprieve to the Graeco-Roman society of the last millennium B.C. A Greek man of letters described Rome's service to this society in an encomium that he wrote in the second half of the second century of the Christian Era, when the Roman Empire was at its zenith. The peoples of the world, so Aelius Aristeides put it, had exhausted themselves in fratricidal struggles until they were all laid out on the funeral pyre, dead and ready to be cremated, but they were resuscitated by the inauguration of the Roman peace. And, in truth, the history of the Mediterranean World during the millennium preceding the establishment of the Roman peace in 31 B.C. had been a history of ever more devastating wars between local sovereign states.

The peace that put an end to these wars prolonged the life of the Graeco-Roman society for five or six more centuries. What happened once at the western end of the Old World, and many times more than once in the world as a whole, can happen again — and now on a world-wide scale.

Aelius Aristeides' eulogy of Rome is impressive evidence of the eventual reconciliation of Rome's subjects to the ideal of a world-state, which was the ideal to which the Roman Empire had given practical, though not truly world-wide, effect. This reconciliation is remarkable, considering that Roman rule had originally been imposed by conquest in the teeth of obstinate resistance, and, down almost to the close of the first century of the Christian Era, Greek men of letters, in the generations preceding Aelius Aristeides' generation, had been the most vocal and eloquent spokesmen of this opposition to political unity.

For at least four centuries, ending with the Emperor Augustus' decisive victory at Actium in 31 B.C., the Mediterranean World had been distracted and devastated progressively by conflicts between local states (city-states, not national states, in this chapter of history). Yet these communities which had been destroying themselves in the process of destroying each other had been bitterly opposed to Rome's high-handed action in forcibly preventing them from committing suicide. Rome had cast her shadow over the Greek World as far back as the second century B.C., but it had taken the Greek intellectuals about a quarter of a millennium to recognize that Rome's suppression of the sovereignty of the historic Greek city-states had been their salvation.

The sequel is more encouraging still. Aelius Aristeides' tribute to Rome's service to the peoples of the Mediterranean World had been paid at a date when the Roman Empire, though still at its height, was on the eve of falling into adversity. The grandchildren of Aelius Aristeides' contemporaries lived to experience the first of the successive convulsions that wrecked the Roman Empire in its backward Western provinces and very nearly wrecked it in the Levant as well. The significant historical fact is that, as soon as the survival of this world-state became uncertain, the eagerness of its subjects to preserve it became wholehearted. Their feeling had already changed from hostility to acquiescence and from acquiescence to gratitude. It now changed to positive loyalty and active concern. The prospect that the world-state might fall to pieces

77

made its subjects poignantly conscious that they could not afford to be deprived of it.

When, in the West, the Roman Empire did go to pieces, the generations that lived through this harrowing experience could not bring themselves to face the fact. Even the barbarians who were carving up the Western provinces into virtually sovereign successor-states preferred, with few exceptions, to legitimize their local rule by exercising it in the name of the Roman world-state, as Rome's local vice-gerents. And when, at last, the demise of the world-state could no longer be ignored, the descendants of its once disaffected subjects joined hands with the descendants of its former barbarian destroyers in successive attempts to re-establish it.

Each of these attempts was a greater failure than its predecessor. In Western Europe (though not in the Levant) the fallen world-state proved to be a Humpty-Dumpty, and, in the thirteenth century, the last attempt to set up the Roman Empire again in the West broke down. Yet the store set on this restoration was so great that the titular existence of the Empire was maintained until 1806, though its effective revival, as an ecumenical state embracing all but a fringe of the Western World, had not outlasted the first Western neo-Roman emperor Charlemagne.

The power that had proved too strong for this abortive restoration had not been national sovereignty, which was to be "the wave of the future," first in the West and eventually in the whole world, but a rival power, the Papacy; and the victory of the Papacy over the Empire had been a victory for one expression of ecumenism over another. The ideal of an all-embracing ecumenical society had maintained itself unimpaired. This shows how strong the hold of ecumenism was over Western hearts down to a date within five and a half centuries of the present.

The medieval Western Christian commonwealth under the presidency of the Papacy was short-lived. In bringing the medieval Western Roman Empire to the ground, the Papacy had undermined the basis of its own authority, which was spiritual, by stooping to the use of physical force. Yet, in its heyday, the Papacy was a Western avatar of the original Roman world-state more effective than the Western-revived Roman Empire had been. The Papal Western Church was a genuine reproduction of the authentic Roman Empire, for the Christian Church had grown up within the Roman Empire and had adopted the Empire's administrative organization as the model for its own. One of the reasons why the Church had proved stronger than the revived Roman Empire in the Middle Ages was that, in this period in the West, there was a famine of educated men, and the lion's share of this limited fund of trained intellectual ability was channeled into the service of the Church, leaving the Empire and the other secular states of the medieval Western World in short supply.

The medieval Western Papacy was more effective than the medieval Western Empire in at least three respects. In the first place, it commanded a more effective administrative apparatus. In the second, its spiritual authority was recognized throughout Western Christendom, whereas the nominal secular authority of the ecumenical Empire was recognized only in Germany, Burgundy, and Northern Italy, and was constantly challenged in fact even where it was recognized officially. In the third place, the spiritual authority of the Papacy was more potent, as long as it retained the respect of the Western World, than the secular authority of the Empire or of any local Western state.

During the prime of the Papacy, secular princes shrank from trying conclusions with it when the two forces came into conflict. They were frightened of a show-down because they were aware that, if their subjects were forced to choose between their secular allegiance to the prince and their spiritual allegiance to the Pope, they were likely to give priority to the latter. When a secular prince was placed under a Papal interdict, his subjects were absolved from their allegiance to him. Indeed, they were under a moral obligation to constrain him to obey the Pope's fiat or, if he refused, to depose him and replace him by a more amenable successor. This was a risk that medieval Western secular princes prudently hesitated to incur. Those who did incur it were apt to suffer humiliation (conspicuous examples are the fates of the Western Roman Emperor Henry IV and the King of England Henry II). When Philip IV of France did summon up the courage to defy Pope Boniface VIII, he was shaking in his shoes. When he convened the French States General, including the French members of the Western clergy, he did not know whether they were going to support him. When they did, he was probably as surprised as he was relieved; as a matter of fact, they might not have supported him if Boniface had not played into Philip's hands by pushing his claim to Papal authority to extravagant lengths.

The defeat of Boniface was only the beginning of the downfall of ecclesiastical ecumenism in the West. The collapse was completed by the Babylonian Captivity, the Great Schism, and the Reformation. The ruin brought with it the eclipse of the ecumenical ideal itself, and the counter-ideal of national sovereignty moved in to occupy the institutional, ideological, and emotional vacuum. For the Western civilization, this resurgence of parochialism has been a grave set-back; and, today, for the world as well, because this Western ideal of national sovereignty has now become the ideal of the whole world as a result of the prestige that the Western way of life has acquired throughout the world.

č

If we were to confine our view to the present moment, the ideal of national sovereignty would fill the whole horizon, and the outlook would be dark, considering that the progress of modern technology has made it imperative to recapture the ecumenical ideal and to embody it rapidly in new institutions of world-wide scope. Fortunately, if we take a longer view — a view embracing the five thousand years that have passed since the emergence of the earliest civilizations — the outlook appears less discouraging. In the perspective given by a survey of these last five thousand years, we can see that the ideal of ecumenical sovereignty has been in the field, in competition with the ideal of fractional sovereignty, since the dawn of civilization.

When the curtain rises on the history of the oldest known civilization — that of the Sumerians in what is now Iraq — we find the Sumerian society fractured politically into a set of local sovereign states. They were city-states, and the same political configuration has recurred in other times and places — for instance, in the Mediterranean World in the last millennium B.C. and in Northern Italy, Flanders, and Germany in the Western Middle Ages. On the other hand, the next oldest known civilization, the Egyptian, started life with the political unification of its whole domain, and this unitary dispensation was maintained, with only occasional lapses, for the next three thousand years — in fact, for the duration of the Egyptian civilization itself.

Moreover, a number of societies whose original political configuration was the fractured one have gone over, in the end, from political plurality to political unity. The Sumerian society was united politically by Akkadian empire-builders and the Greek society by the Romans. The Chinese society, which started life politically as a set of "warring states," was unified politically in 221 B.C., two centuries earlier than the contemporary Greek World; and, once united, China has remained united (though, like Egypt, with occasional temporary relapses into disunity) from 221 B.C. until the present day.

What are the modern world's chances of such political unification? The most obvious of the driving forces making for unification is the progress of technology. This has now made war suicidal, while it has put a premium on the maximum scale of operations for constructive purposes. If the present generation of mankind has the will to replace national sovereignty by world government, present-day technology offers it ample material means, far more potent than those which any previous generation has had at its command. But this fact indicates that, for establishing world government, the will is all-important, and the material means, however effective, are only a secondary factor, for the Egyptians, Sumerians, Greeks, Chinese, and Peruvians all succeeeded in achieving political unity — on scales that were large even by modern standards — despite the fact that their technological equipment was not only immeasurably inferior to ours but was no better under their ecumenical regimes than it had been when they had been living in small-scale local sovereign states.

The Roman Empire in the second century of the Christian era did not possess any better means of communication than had been possessed by the hundreds of local sovereign city-states into which the same area had been previously divided in the seventh and sixth centuries B.C. The change that had made the political revolution possible had not been a change in the field of technology; it had been a change of heart; and this change of heart had been produced by painful experience.

Let us make the hazardous assumption that we, in our turn, are going to achieve the same change of heart for the same reason. On this assumption, how are we likely to organize a literally world-wide world government under modern technological and social conditions? We may perhaps guess that a future world community will have a dual political structure. It will have a territorial structure of the traditional kind, but this will be supplemented, and will eventually be overshadowed, by the functional structure that has now been made feasible by technology's recent feat of "annihilating distance."

It seems fairly safe to forecast that, if the human race survives, it will have abandoned the ideal and the practice of national sovereignty. This does not necessarily involve the liquidation of national units of local administration. On the contrary, their survival, no longer as sovereign states but as subordinate organs of local self-government, seems to be assured by several considerations.

In the first place, the invention of the atomic weapon has ruled out the traditional method of political unification by military conquest; unification can be brought about only voluntarily, by mutual consent. This means that a future world-state will, in one of its aspects, inevitably take the form of a federal state whose constituent members will be the states that, today, are sovereign bodies. Of course, the price of federation will be the forfeiture of their sovereignty in fact, but they are likely to be subordinated, not liquidated. It may even be politic to appease national sentiment by allowing states to retain the title "sovereign." The title will be harmless so long as it is made meaningless. After all, the fifty states of the United States are, each and all, officially sovereign, but the supremacy of the Federal government over them is not inhibited by that.

In the second place, the national states of the world can serve a useful purpose, for, even in an age in which technology has "annihilated distance," some branches of public administration, such as the management of some public utilities, are intrinsically local. It is true that we can pipe water, gas, and oil, and can transmit electric power over immense distances, and we can foresee the day at which the optimum territorial unit for the administration of these public services will no longer be a county or even a national state but nothing less than a whole continent. However, we are still left with the drains. It is hard to imagine that the network of services can be operated on a scale larger than a national one. So the national units will have at least one indispensable public utility left for them to administer. Today, the national state is a god (for sovereignty, when one analyzes its implications, means divinity, nothing less). Tomorrow, this god may be reduced to justifying his existence by minding the drains. The national state will not have been the only historic institution that has come down in the world so precipitously.

č

The most important future territorial unit is likely to be the smallest one of all. The coming world is going to be a world of streets and houses, a globe-encompassing ecumenopolis; and, to keep life human in this vast impersonal termitary, it will be necessary to plan the world-city as an aggregate of an immense number of distinct units, each of which will be on a small enough scale to make it possible for its inhabitants to be each other's neighbors in the sense of being personally acquainted with each other.

This was the scale of Neolithic Jericho and early nineteenth-century Weimar, as Weimar still was in Goethe's old age. It is the scale of the units in which the Muslim refugees from India have been re-housed in the environs of Karachi on a plan worked out by the Greek planner Konstandinos Doxiadis. It is also the scale of a quadro in Lucio Costa's Brasilia. (A quadro is a unit in which a family can live and in which the women can do their shopping and washing and the children can go to school without having to cross roads infested with power-driven traffic.) This minimum-sized territorial unit, small enough to be able to satisfy the basic human need for personal relations of neighborliness, will assume even greater social importance as ecumenopolis proliferates. To be genuine neighbors, people — and perhaps especially women and children — must live within walking distance of each other. This is a permanent fact of human nature: it holds good under all conditions — not only when human feet are the only means of human locomotion but also when distance has been "annihilated" by the possibility of being catapulted around the globe in supersonic jet planes.

This is true of personal relations. However, in human social life impersonal relations are also important. For these, "the annihilation of distance" is going to make geographical proximity irrelevant. For, besides being members of our family circle and our tiny company of personal friends, we are also involved in networks of impersonal relations on a large scale. We are colleagues of people who follow the same profession; we are co-religionists of people who are adherents of the same church. In these impersonal capacities, we have always been in relations with people far beyond the limits of our family circle. In a world-wide society that has achieved "the annihilation of distance," there will be no limit to the range of these impersonal relations short of the limits of mankind's total habitat.

We are within sight of a time when Buddhists, pigeon-fanciers, morticians, Methodists, stamp-collectors, bird-watchers, physicists, lawyers, Roman Catholics, bankers, oilmen, and an almost endless list of other sets of people who are drawn together by some common interest will be organizing themselves on a world-wide scale.

The bankers, oilmen, Catholics, stamp-collectors, and some others have gone far towards achieving this world-wideness already. Conventions and congresses attended by delegates from all around the globe are frequent; and it can be foreseen that, in an age in which distance is no longer an impediment to meeting, this functional organization of human affairs will rival in importance, and perhaps eventually overshadow, the local organization which necessarily prevailed so long as communications were a problem. In the future world, with a population three, four, or ten times as large as the present world's population, the problem will be congestion; and we can imagine a stage at which people will do world-wide business of all kinds with each other by telephone, radio, and television without any physical displacement of human bodies. In any case the functional organization of human affairs is going to play a major part in the coming world order of mankind.

It is a far cry from local sovereign national states to international functional associations, each of which will have its members scattered over the whole face of the earth and will take the whole world for its field. World-wide functional associations for all kinds of purposes may become the mainstay of the political as well as the economic, social, and cultural organization of the human race when mankind has coalesced into a single world-wide society living under a single world-wide government. This should be our goal, and we should be straining every nerve to reach it. We have far to go and we have little time.

Since 1945, "time's wingèd chariot hurrying near" has been loaded with the atom bomb. The task of the present generation is to put the out-of-date sovereign national state in its place before one of the chronic conflicts between these antediluvian monsters releases the precarious catch that holds the bomb back from dropping. ❧

The Open Truth
and Fiery Vehemence
of Youth

PETER MARIN

It is midnight and I am sitting here with my notes,
enough of them to make two books and a half and a
volume of posthumous fragments, trying to make
some smaller sense of them than the grand maniacal
design I have in my mind. I don't know where to begin. Once, traveling in summer across the country
with a friend from Hollywood and my young son in
a battered green Porsche, I stopped for lunch somewhere in Kansas on a Sunday morning. As we walked
into the restaurant, bearded, wearing dark glasses
and strange hats, and followed by my long-haired
boy, one Kansas matron bent toward another and
whispered: "I bet those two men have kidnapped
that little girl." I took a deep breath and started to
speak, but I did not know where to begin or how to
explain just how many ways she was mistaken. Now,
trying to write clearly about education and adolescence, I feel the same way.

For that reason I have chosen an eccentric method
of composition, one that may seem fragmentary,
jumpy, and broken. This article will be more like a

letter, and the letter itself is an accumulation of impressions and ideas, a sampling of thoughts at once disconnected but related. There is a method to it that may disappear in its mild madness, but I do not know at this juncture how else to proceed. Shuffling through my notes I feel like an archeologist with a mass of uncatalogued shards. There is a pattern to all this, a coherence of thought, but all I can do here is assemble the bits and pieces and lay them out for you and hope that you can sense how I get from one place to another.

An entire system is hiding behind this, just beginning to take form, and these notes are like a drawing, a preliminary sketch. I feel comfortable with that notion, more comfortable than with the idea of forcing them together, cutting and pasting, to make a more conventional essay. I can perceive in myself at this moment what I also see in the young: I am reluctant to deal in sequence with my ideas and experience, I am impatient with transition, the habitual ways of getting "from here to there." I think restlessly; my mind, like the minds of my students, works in flashes, in sudden perceptions and brief extended clusters of intuition and abstraction—and I have stuck stubbornly to that method of composition. There is still in me the ghost of an apocalyptic adolescent, and I am trying to move it a few steps toward the future.

One theme, as you will see, runs through what I have written or thought: we must rethink our ideas of childhood and schooling. We must dismantle them and start again from scratch. Nothing else will do. Our visions of adolescence and education confine us to habit, rule perception out. We make do at the moment with a set of ideas inherited from the nineteenth century, from an industrial, relatively puritanical, repressive, and "localized" culture; we try to gum them like labels to new kinds of experience. But that won't do. Everything has changed. The notions with which I began my job as a high-school director have been discarded one by one. They make no sense. What emerges through these children as the psyche of this culture is post-industrial, relatively unrepressed, less literate and local: a new combination of elements, almost a new strain. Adolescents are, each one of them, an arena in which the culture transforms itself or is torn between contrary impulses; they are the victims of a culture raging within itself like man and wife, a schizoid culture—and these children are the unfinished and grotesque products of that schism.

They are grotesque because we give them no help. They are forced to make among themselves adjustments to a tension that must be unbearable. They do the best they can, trying, in increasingly eccentric fashions, to make sense of things. But we adults seem to have withdrawn in defeat from that same struggle, to have given up. We are enamored, fascinated, and deluded by adolescence precisely because it is the last life left to us; only the young rebel with any real passion against media, machines, the press of circumstance itself. Their elders seem to have no options, no sense of alternative or growth. Adult existence is bled of life and we turn in that vacuum toward children with the mixed repulsion and desire of wanton Puritans toward life itself.

As for me, an adult, I think of myself as I write as an observer at a tribal war—an anthropologist, a combination of Gulliver and a correspondent sending home news by mule and boat. By the time you hear of it, things will have changed. And that isn't enough, not enough at all. Somebody must step past the children, must move into his own psyche or two steps past his own limits into the absolute landscape of fear and potential these children inhabit. That is where I am headed. So these ideas, in effect, are something like a last message tacked to a tree in a thicket or tucked under a stone. I mean: we cannot *follow* the children any longer, we have to step ahead of them. Somebody has to mark a trail.

౿

Adolescence: a few preliminary fragments . . .

(FROM MY STUDENT, V): *yr whole body moves in a trained way & you know that youve moved this way before & it contains all youve been taught its all rusty & slow something is pushing under that rusted mesh but STILL YOU CANNOT MOVE you are caught between 2 doors & the old one is much closer & you can grab it all the time but the other door it disappears that door you cant even scratch & kick (like the early settlers were stung by the new land) but this new land doesnt even touch you & you wonder if youre doing the right thing to get in*

(FROM FRANZ KAFKA): *He feels imprisoned on this earth, he feels constricted; the melancholy, the impotence, the sicknesses, the feverish fancies of the captive afflict him; no comfort can comfort him, since it is merely comfort, gentle headsplitting comfort glazing the brutal fact of imprisonment. But if he is asked what he wants he cannot reply. . . . He has no conception of freedom.*

(FROM TAPES RECORDED IN PACIFIC PALISADES, 1966, SEVERAL BOYS AND GIRLS AGED 12-14):—*Things are getting younger and younger. Girls twelve will do it*

now. One guy said I fuck a girl every Friday night.
What sexual pleasure do you get out of this (he's very
immature you know) and he would say, I don't know
I'm just going to fuck.

or

—How old are you?   —*Twelve.*   —Will you tell us
your first experience with drugs, how you got into it?
—*Well, the people I hung around with were big acid-*
heads. So one day my friend asked me if I wanted to
get stoned and I said yes. That was about five months
ago and I've been getting on it every since. Started
taking LSD about one month ago. Took it eleven
times in one month. I consider it a good thing. For
getting high, smoking grass is better, or hashish—it's
about six times stronger than marijuana.

(FROM PAUL RADIN: Primitive Man As Philosopher):
It is conceivably demanding too much of a man to
whom the pleasures of life are largely bound up with
the life of contemplation and to whom analysis and
introspection are the self-understood prerequisites for
a proper understanding of the world, that he appre-
ciate . . . expressions which are largely non-intellectual
—where life seems, predominatingly, a discharge of
physical vitality, a simple and naive release of emo-
tions or an enjoyment of sensations for their own
sake. Yet . . . it is just such an absorption in a life of
sensations that is the outward characteristic of primi-
tive peoples.

Can you see where my thought leads? It is precisely
at this point, adolescence, when the rush of energies,
that sea-sex, gravitation, the thrust of the ego up
through layers of childhood, makes itself felt, that the
person is once more like an infant, is swept once

more by energies that are tidal, unfamiliar, and unyielding. He is in a sense born again, a fresh identity beset inside and out by the rush of new experience. It is at this point, too—when we seem compelled by a persistent lunacy to isolate him—that what is growing within the adolescent demands expression, requires it, and must, in addition, be received by the world and given form—or it will wither or turn to rage. Adolescence is a second infancy. It is then that a man desires solitude and at the same time contact with the vivid world; must test within social reality the new power within himself; needs above all to discover himself for the first time as a bridge between inner and outer, a maker of value, a vehicle through which culture perceives and transforms itself. It is now, ideally, that he begins to understand the complex and delicate nature of the ego itself as a thin skin between living worlds, a synaptic jump, the self-conscious point at which nature and culture combine.

In this condition, with these needs, the adolescent is like a primitive man, an apocalyptic primitive; he exists for the moment in that stage of single vision in which myth is still the raw stuff of being, he knows at first hand through his own energies the possibilities of life—but he knows these in muddled, sporadic, contradictory ways. The rush of his pubescent and raw energy seems at odds with public behavior, the *order* of things, the tenor of life around him, especially in a culture just emerging—as is ours—from a tradition of evasion, repression, and fear.

The contradictions within the culture itself intensify his individual confusion. We are at the moment torn between future and past: in the midst of a process of transformation we barely understand. The development of adolescent energy and ego—difficult at any time—is complicated in our own by the increase in early sexuality, the complicated messages of the media, and the effects of strong and unfamiliar drugs. These three elements are, in themselves, the salient features of a culture that is growing more permissive, less repressive. They are profound, complex, and strong: heavy doses of experience demanding changes in attitude, changes in behavior. The direction and depth of feeling responds accordingly; the adolescent tries—even as a form of self-defense against the pressure of his own energies—to move more freely, to change his styles of life, to "grow." But it is then that he finds he is locked into culture, trapped in a web of ideas, law, and rituals that keep him a child, deprive him of a chance to test and assimilate his newer self. It is now that the culture turns suddenly repressive. His gestures are evaded or denied; at best he is "tolerated," but even then his gestures, lacking the social support of acknowledgment and reward, must seem to him lacking in authenticity—more like forms of neurosis or selfishness than the natural stages in growth.

He is thrust back upon himself. The insistent natural press within him toward becoming whole is met perpetually by unbudging resistance. Schools, rooted as they are in a Victorian century and seemingly suspicious of life itself, are his natural enemies. They don't help, as they might, to make that bridge between his private and the social worlds; they insist, instead, upon their separation. Indeed, family, community, and school all combine—especially in the suburbs—to isolate and "protect" him from the adventure, risk, and participation he needs; the same energies that relate him at this crucial point to nature result in a kind of exile from the social environment.

Thus the young, in that vivid confrontation with the thrust of nature unfolding in themselves, are denied adult assistance. I once wrote that education through its limits denied the gods, and that they would return in the young in one form or another to haunt us. That is happening now. You can sense it as the students gather, with their simplistic moral certainty, at the gates of the universities. It is almost as if the young were once more possessed by Bacchanalian gods, were once again inhabited by divinities whose honor we have neglected. Those marvelous and threatening energies! What disturbs me most about them is that we lack rituals for their use and balance, and the young—and perhaps we ourselves—now seem at their mercy. The young have moved, bag and baggage, into areas where adults cannot help them, and it is a scary landscape they face, it is crowded with strange forms and faces, and if they return from it raddled, without balance and pitched toward excess, who can pretend to be surprised—or blameless?

At times they seem almost shell-shocked, survivors of a holocaust in which the past has been destroyed and all the bridges to it bombed. I cannot describe with any certainty what occurs in their minds, but I do know that most adults must seem to the young like shrill critics speaking to them in an alien language about a Greek tragedy in which they may lose their lives. The words we use, our dress, our tones of voice, the styles of adult lives—all of these are so foreign to that dramatic crisis that as we approach them we seem to increase the distance we are trying to cross. Even our attention drives them further away, as if adolescents perceived that adults, coming closer, diminish in sense and size.

The inner events in an adolescent demand from what surrounds him life on a large scale, in a grand style. This is the impulse to apocalypse in the young, as if they were in exile from a nation that does not exist—and yet they can sense it, they know it is there —if only because their belief itself demands its presence. Their demand is absolute and unanswerable, but it exists and we seem unable at this point in time to suppress or evade it. For one reason or another, massive shifts in cultural balances, the lessening of repression for whatever reasons—economic, technological, evolutionary—those energies, like gods, have appeared among us again. But what can we make of them? The simple problem is that our institutions are geared to another century, another set of social necessities, and cannot change quickly enough to contain, receive, or direct them—and as we suppress or refuse them they turn to rage.

᷍
č

Primitive cultures dealt with this problem, I think, through their initiation rites, the rites of passage; they legitimized and accepted these energies and turned them toward collective aims; they were merged with the life of the tribe and in this way acknowledged, honored, and domesticated—but not destroyed. In most initiation rites the participant is led through the mythical or sacred world (or a symbolic version) and is then returned, transformed, to the secular one as a new person, with a new role. He is introduced through the rites to a dramatic reality coexistent with the visible or social one and at its root; he is put in direct touch with the sources of energy, the divinities of the tribe. In many cultures the symbolic figures in the rites are unmasked at the end, as if to reveal to the initiate the interpenetration of the secular and sacred worlds. Occasionally the initiate is asked at some point to don the ritual mask himself—joining, as he does, one world with another and assuming the responsibility for their connection. This shift in status, in *relation*, is the heart of the rite; a liturgized merging of the individual with shared sources of power.

Do you see what I am driving at? The rites are in a sense a social contract, a binding up; one occurring specifically, profoundly, on a deep psychic level. The individual is redefined in the culture by his new relation to its mysteries, its gods, to one form or another of nature. His experience of that hidden and omnipotent mythical world is the basis for his relation to the culture and his fellows, each of whom has a similar bond—deep, personal, and unique, but somehow shared, invisibly but deeply. These ritualized relationships of each man to the shared gods bind the group together; they form the substance of culture: an invisible landscape that is real and felt, commonly held, a landscape which resides in each man and in which, in turn, each man resides.

I hope that makes sense. That is the structure of the kaleidoscopic turning of culture that Blake makes in "The Crystal Cabinet," and it makes sense too, in America, in relation to adolescents. What fascinates me is that our public schools, designed for adolescents —who seem, as apocalyptic men, to demand this kind of drama, release, and support—educate and "socialize" their students by depriving them of everything the rites bestow. They manipulate them through the repression of energies; they isolate them and close off most parts of the community; they categorically refuse to make use of the individual's private experience. The direction of all these tendencies is toward a cultural schizophrenia in which the student is forced to choose between his own relation to reality or the one demanded by the institution. The schools are organized to weaken the student so that he is forced, in the absence of his own energies, to accept the values and demands of the institution. To this end we deprive the student of mobility and experience; through law and custom we make the only legal place for him the school, and then, to make sure he remains dependent, manipulable, we empty the school of all vivid life.

We appear to have forgotten in our schools what every primitive tribe with its functional psychology knows: allegiance to the tribe can be forged only at the deepest levels of the psyche and in extreme circumstance demanding endurance, daring, and awe; that the participant must be given *direct* access to the sources of cultural continuity—by and in himself; and that only a place in a coherent community can be exchanged for a man's allegiance.

I believe that it is precisely this world that drugs replace; adolescents provide for themselves what we deny them: a confrontation with some kind of power within an unfamiliar landscape involving sensation and risk. It is there, I suppose, that they hope to find, by some hurried magic, a new way of seeing, a new relation to things, to discard one identity and assume another. They mean to find through their adventures the *ground* of reality, the resonance of life we deny them, as if they might come upon their golden city and return still inside it: at home. You can see the real veterans sometimes on the street in strange costumes they have stolen from dreams: American versions of the Tupi of Brazil, who traveled thousands of miles each year in search of the land where death and evil do not exist. Theirs is a world totally alien to the one we discuss in schools; it is dramatic, it enchants them; its existence forms a strange brotherhood among them and they cling to it—as though they alone had been to a fierce land and back. It is that which draws them together and makes of them a loose tribe. It is, after all, some sort of shared experience, some kind of foray into the risky dark; it is the best that they can do.

❦

When you begin to think about adolescence in this way, what sense can you make of our schools? None of the proposed changes makes sense to me: revision of curriculum, teaching machines, smaller classes, encounter groups, redistributions of power—all of these are stopgap measures, desperate attempts to keep the young in schools that are hopelessly outdated. The changes suggested and debated don't go deeply enough; they don't question or change enough. For what needs changing are not the methods of the school system but its aims, and what is troubling the young and forcing upon their teachers an intolerable burden is the *idea* of childhood itself; the ways we think about adolescents, their place in the culture itself. More and more one comes to see that changes in the schools won't be enough; the crisis of the young cuts across the culture in all its areas and includes the family and the community. The young are displaced; there seems no other word for it. They are trapped in a prolonged childhood almost unique.

In few other cultures have persons of fifteen or eighteen been so uselessly isolated from participation in the community, or been deemed so unnecessary (in their elders' eyes), or so limited by law. Our ideas of responsibility, our parental feelings of anxiety, blame, and guilt, all of these follow from our curious vision of the young; in turn, they concretize it, legitimize it so that we are no longer even conscious of the ways we see childhood or the strain that our vision puts upon us. That is what needs changing: the definitions we make socially and legally of the role of the young. They are trapped in the ways we see them, and the school is simply one function, one aspect, of the whole problem. What makes real change so difficult in the schools is only in part their natural unwieldiness; it is more often the difficulty we have in escaping our preconceptions about things.

In general the school system we have inherited seems to me based upon three particular things:

☐ What Paul Goodman calls the idea of "natural depravity": our puritanical vision of human nature in which children are perceived as sinners or "savages" and in which human impulse or desire is not to be trusted and must therefore be constrained or "trained."

☐ The necessity during the mid-nineteenth century of "Americanizing" great masses of immigrant children from diverse backgrounds and creating, through the schools, a common experience and character.

☐ The need in an industrialized state for energy and labor to run the machines: the state, needing workers, educates persons to be technically capable but relatively dependent and responsive to authority so that their energies will be available when needed.

These elements combine with others—the labor laws that make childhood a "legal" state, and a population explosion that makes it necessary now to keep adolescents off both the labor market and the idle street—to "freeze" into a school system that resists change even as the culture itself and its needs shift radically. But teachers can't usually see that, for they themselves have been educated in this system and are committed to ideas that they have never clearly understood. Time and again, speaking to them, one hears the same questions and anguish:

"But what will happen to the students if they don't go to school?" "How will they learn?" "What will they do without adults?"

What never comes clear, of course, is that such questions are, at bottom, statement. Even while asking them teachers reveal their unconscious and contaminating attitudes. They can no longer imagine what children will do "outside" schools. They regard them as young monsters who will, if released from adult authority or help, disrupt the order of things. What is more, adults no longer are capable of imagining learning or child-adult relationships outside the schools. But mass schooling is a recent innovation. Most learning—especially the process of socialization or acculturation—has gone on outside schools, more naturally, in the fabric of the culture. In most cultures the passage from childhood to maturity occurs because of social necessity, the need for responsible adults, and is marked by clear changes in role. Children in the past seem to have learned the ways of the community or tribe through constant contact and interchange with adults, and it was taken for granted that the young learned continually through their place close to the heart of the community.

We seem to have lost all sense of that. The school is expected to do what the community cannot do and that is impossible. In the end, we will have to change far more than the schools if we expect to create a new coherence between the experiences of the child and the needs of the community. We will have to rethink the meaning of childhood; we will begin to grant greater freedom *and* responsibility to the young; we will drop the compulsory-schooling age to fourteen, perhaps less; we will take for granted the "independence" of adolescents and provide them with the chance to live alone, away from parents and with peers; we will discover jobs they can or want to do in the community—anything from mail delivery to the teaching of smaller children and the counseling of other adolescents. At some point, perhaps, we will even find that the community itself—in return for a minimum of work or continued schooling—will provide a minimal income to young people that will allow them to assume the responsibility for their own lives at an earlier age, and learn the ways of the community outside the school; finally, having lowered the level of compulsory schooling, we will find it necessary to provide different *kinds* of schools, a wider choice, so that students will be willing voluntarily to continue the schooling that suits their needs and aims.

All these changes, of course, are aimed at two things: the restoration of the child's "natural" place in the community and lowering the age at which a person is considered an independent member of the community. Some of them, to be sure, can be made in the schools, but my sense of things, after having talked to teachers and visited the schools, is that trying to make the changes in schools *alone* will be impossible.

One problem, put simply, is that in every school I have visited, public or private, traditional or "innovational," the students have only these two choices: to drop out (either physically or mentally) or to make themselves smaller and smaller until they can act in ways their elders expect. One of my students picked up a phrase I once used, "the larger and smaller worlds." The schools we visit together, he says, are always the smaller world: smaller at least than his imagination, smaller than the potential of the young. The students are asked to put aside the best things about themselves—their own desires, impulses, and ideas—in order to "adjust" to an environment constructed for children who existed one hundred years ago, if at all. I wonder sometimes if this condition is simply the result of poor schooling; I am more inclined to believe that it is the inevitable result of mass compulsory schooling and the fabrication of artificial environments by adults for children. Is it possible at all for adults to understand what children need and to change their institutions fast enough to keep up with changes in culture and experience? Is it possible for children to grow to their full size, to feel their full strength, if they are deprived of individual volition all along the line and forced to school? I don't know. I know only that during the Middle Ages they sometimes "created" jesters by putting young children in boxes and force-feeding them so that, as they grew, their bones would warp in unusual shapes. That is often how the schools seem to me. Students are trapped in the boxes of pedagogic ideas, and I am tempted to say to teachers again and again: more, much more, you must go further, create more space in the schools, you must go deeper in thought, create more resonance, a different feeling, a different and more human, more daring style.

Even the best teachers, with the best intentions, seem to diminish their students as they work through the public-school system. For that system is, at bottom, designed to produce what we sometimes call good citizens but what more often than not turn out to be good soldiers; it is through the schools of the state, after all, that we produce our armies. I remember how struck I was while teaching at a state college by the number of boys who wanted to oppose the draft but lacked the courage or strength to simply say no. They were trapped; they had always been taught, had always tried, to be "good." Now that they wanted to refuse to go, they could not, for they weren't sure they could bear the consequences they had been taught would follow such refusal: jail, social disgrace, loss of jobs, parental despair. They could not believe in institutions, but they could not trust themselves and their impulse and they were caught in their own impotence: depressed and resentful, filled with self-hatred and a sense of shame.

That is a condition bred in the schools. In one way or another our methods produce in the young a condition of pain that seems very close to a mass neurosis: a lack of faith in oneself, a vacuum of spirit into which authority or institutions can move, a dependency they feed on. Students are encouraged to relinquish their own wills, their freedom of volition; they are taught that value and culture reside outside oneself and must be acquired from the institution, and almost everything in their education is designed to discourage them from activity, from the wedding of idea and act. It is almost as if we hoped to discourage them from thought itself by making ideas so lifeless, so hopeless, that their despair would be enough to make them manipulable and obedient.

The system breeds obedience, frustration, dependence, and fear: a kind of gentle violence that is usually turned against oneself, one that is sorrowful and full of guilt, but a violence nonetheless, and one realizes that what is done in the schools to persons is deeply connected to what we did to the blacks or are doing now in Vietnam. That is: we don't teach hate in the schools, or murder, but we do isolate the individual; we empty him of life by ignoring or suppressing his impulse toward life; we breed in him a lack of respect for it, a loss of love—and thus we produce gently "good" but threatened men, men who will kill without passion, out of duty and obedience, men who have in themselves little sense of the vivid life being lost nor the moral strength to refuse.

From first to twelfth grade we acclimatize students to a fundamental deadness and teach them to restrain themselves for the sake of "order." The net result is a kind of pervasive cultural inversion in which they are asked to separate at the most profound levels their own experience from institutional reality, self from society, objective from subjective, energy from order —though these various polarities are precisely those which must be made coherent during adolescence.

I remember a talk I had with a college student.

"You know what I love to do," he said. "I love to go into the woods and run among the trees."

"Very nice," I said.

"But it worries me. We shouldn't do it."

"Why not?" I asked.

"Because we get excited. It isn't *orderly*."

"Not orderly?"

"Not orderly."

"Do you run into the trees?" I asked.

"Of course not."

"Then it's orderly," I said.

In a small way this exchange indicates the kind of thinking we encourage in the schools: the mistaking of rigidity and stillness for order, of order as the absence of life. We try to create and preserve an order which depends upon the destruction of life both inside and out and which all life, when expressed, must necessarily threaten or weaken.

The natural process of learning seems to move naturally from experience through perception to abstraction in a fluid continuous process that cannot be clearly divided into stages. It is in that process that energy is somehow articulated in coherent and meaningful form as an act or thought or a made object. The end of learning is wisdom and wisdom to me, falling back as I do on a Jewish tradition, is, in its simplest sense, "intelligent activity" or, more completely, the suffusion of activity with knowledge, a wedding of the two. For the Hassidic Jews every gesture was potentially holy, a form of prayer, when it was made with a reverence for God. In the same way a gesture is always a form of wisdom—an act is wisdom—when it is suffused with knowledge, made with a reverence for the truth.

Does that sound rhetorical? I suppose it does. But I mean it. The end of education is intelligent activity, *wisdom,* and that demands a merging of opposites, a sense of process. Instead we produce the opposite: immobility, insecurity, an inability to act without institutional blessing or direction, or, at the opposite pole, a headlong rush toward motion without balance or thought. We cut into the natural movement of learning and try to force upon the students the end product, abstraction, while eliminating experience and ignoring their perception. The beginning of thought is in the experience through one's self of a particular environment—school, community, culture. When this is ignored, as it is in schools, the natural relation of self and knowledge is broken, the parts of the process become polar opposites, antitheses, and the young are forced to choose between them: objectivity, order, and obedience as against subjectivity, chaos, and energy. It doesn't really matter which they choose; as long as the two sets seem irreconcilable their learning remains incomplete. Caught between the two, they suffer our intellectual schizophrenia until it occupies them, too. They wait. They sit. They listen. They learn to "behave" at the expense of themselves. Or else—and you can see it happening now—they turn against it with a vengeance and may shout, as they did at Columbia, "Kill all adults," for they have allied themselves with raw energy against reason and balance—our delicate, hard-won virtues—and we should not be surprised. We set up the choices ourselves, and it is simply that they have chosen what we hold to be the Devil's side.

೭

If this is the case, what are the alternatives? I thought at one time that changes in schooling could be made, that the school itself could become at least a microcosm of the community outside, a kind of halfway house, a preparatory arena in which students, in semi-protective surroundings, would develop not only the skill but the character that would be needed in the world. But more and more, as I have said, it seems to me impossible to do that job in a setting as isolated and restrictive as our schools. Students don't need the artificiality of schools; they respond more fully and more intelligently when they make direct contact with the community and are allowed to choose roles that have some utility for the community and themselves. What is at stake here, I suppose, is the freedom of volition, for this is the basic condition with which people must learn to deal, and the sooner they achieve within that condition wit, daring, and responsibility the stronger they will be. It seems absurd to postpone the assumption of that condition as long as we do. In most other cultures, and even in our own past, young people have taken upon themselves the responsibility of adults and have dealt with it as successfully as most adults do now. The students I have seen can do that, too, when given the chance. What a strain it must be to have that capacity, to sense in one's self a talent for adventure or growth or meaning, and have that sense continually stifled or undercut by the role one is supposed to play.

Thus, it seems inescapably clear that our first obligation to the young is to create a place in the community for them to act with volition and freedom. They are ready for it, certainly, even if we aren't. Adolescents seem to need at least some sense of risk and gain "out there" in the world: an existential sense of themselves that is vivid to the extent that the dangers faced are "real." The students I have worked with seem strongest and most alive when they are in the mountains of Mexico or the Oakland ghetto or out in the desert or simply hitchhiking or riding freights to see what's happening. They thrive on distance and motion—and the right to solitude when they want it. Many of them want jobs; they themselves arrange to be teachers in day-care centers, political canvassers, tutors, poolroom attendants, actors, governesses, gardeners. They returned from these experiences immeasurably brightened and more sure of themselves, more willing, in that new assurance, to learn many of the abstract ideas we had been straining to teach them. It was not simply the experience in itself that brought this about. It was also the feeling of freedom they had, the sense that they could come and go at will and make any choice they wanted—no matter how absurd—if they were willing to suffer what real consequences followed. Many wanted to work and travel and others did not; they wanted to sit and think or read or live alone or swim or, as one student scrawled on my office wall, "ball and goof." What they finally came to understand, of course, was that the school made no pretense at either limiting or judging their activities; we considered them free agents and limited our own activities to advice, to what "teaching" they requested, and to support when they needed it in facing community, parents, or law.

What we were after was a *feeling* to the place: a sense of intensity and space. We discarded the idea of the microcosm and replaced it with an increased openness and access to the larger community. The campus itself became a place to come back to for rest or discussion or thought; but we turned things inside out to the extent that we came to accept that learning took place more naturally elsewhere, in any of the activities that our students chose, and that the school was in actuality wherever they were, whatever they did. What students learned at the school was simply the feel of things; the sense of themselves as makers of value; the realization that the environment is at best an extension of men and that it can be or meaning, and have that sense continually stifled or undercut by the role one is supposed to play.

Thus, it seems inescapably clear that our first obligation to the young is to create a place in the community for them to act with volition and freedom. They are ready for it, certainly, even if we aren't. Adolescents seem to need at least some sense of risk and gain "out there" in the world: an existential sense of themselves that is vivid to the extent that the dangers faced are "real." The students I have worked with seem strongest and most alive when they are in the mountains of Mexico or the Oakland ghetto or out in the desert or simply hitchhiking or riding freights to see what's happening. They thrive on distance and motion—and the right to solitude when they want it. Many of them want jobs; they themselves arrange to be teachers in day-care centers, political canvassers, tutors, poolroom attendants, actors, governesses, gardeners. They returned from these experiences immeasurably brightened and more sure introspection in which they appeared to grow mysteriously, almost like plants. But an even greater number seemed to need independent commerce with the world outside the school: new sorts of social existence. Nothing could replace that. The simple fact seemed to be that our students grew when they were allowed to move freely into and around the adult community; when they were not, they languished.

We came to see that learning is natural, yes, but it results naturally from most things adolescents do. By associating learning with one particular form of intellection and insisting upon that in school we make a grave error. When students shy away from that kind of intellection it doesn't mean they are turning away forever from learning or abstractions; it means simply that they are seeking another kind of learning momentarily more natural to themselves. That may be anything from physical adventure or experimental community work to withdrawn introspection and an exploration of their fantasies and dreams.

Indeed, it is hard for them to do anything without some kind of learning, but that may be what we secretly fear—that those other forms of learning will make them less manageable or less like ourselves. That, after all, may be one reason we use all those books. Levi-Strauss insists on the relation of increased literacy and the power of the state over the individual. It may well be that dependence on print and abstraction is one of the devices we use to make students manipulable, as if we meant to teach them that ideas exist in talk or on the page but rarely in activity. We tried to avoid that. When we permitted students the freedom of choice and gave them easy access to the community, we found that ideas acquired weight and value to the extent that students were allowed to try them out in action. It was in practical and social situations that their own strength increased, and the merging of the two—strengthened self and tested knowledge—moved them more quickly toward manhood than anything else I have seen.

One might make a formula of it: to the extent that students had freedom of volition and access to experience knowledge became important. But volition and access were of absolute value; they took precedence over books or parental anxiety; without them, nothing worked. So we had to trust the students to make their own choices, no matter what we thought of them. We learned to take their risks with them—and to survive. In that sense we became equals, and that equality may in the end be more educational for students than anything else. That, in fact, may be the most important thing we learned. New ways in seeing them were more effective than changes in curriculum, and without them nothing made much difference. But we must understand too that the old way of seeing things—the traditional idea of childhood—is in some way baked into the whole public-school system at almost every level and also hidden in most pedagogy.

In some ways it is compulsory schooling itself which is the problem, for without real choice students will remain locked in childhood and schools, away from whatever is vivid in life. But real choice, as we know, includes dominion over one's own time and energies, and the right to come and go on the basis of what has actual importance. And I wonder if we will ever get round, given all our fears, to granting that privilege to students.

🍂

One thing alone of all I have read has made recent sense to me concerning adolescents. That is the implicit suggestion in Erik Erikson's *Young Man Luther* that every sensitive man experiences in himself the conflicts and contradictions of his age. The great man, he suggests, is the man who articulates and resolves these conflicts in a way that has meaning for his time; that is, he is himself, as was Luther, a victim of his time and its vehicle and, finally, a kind of resolution. But all men, not only the great, have in some measure the capacity to experience in themselves what is happening in the culture around them. I am talking here about what is really shared among the members of a particular culture is a condition, a kind of internal "landscape," the psychic shape that a particular time and place assumes within a man as the extent and limit of his perceptions, dreams, and pleasure and pain.

If there is such a shared condition it seems to me a crucial point, for it means that there is never any real distance between a man and his culture, no real isolation or alienation from society. It means that adolescents are not in their untutored state cut off from culture nor outside it. It means instead that each adolescent is an arena in which the contradictions and currents sweeping through the culture must somehow be resolved, must be resolved by the person himself, and that those individual resolutions are, ideally, the means by which the culture advances itself.

Do you see where this leads? I am straining here to get past the idea of the adolescent as an isolate and deviant creature who must be joined—as if glued and clamped—to the culture. For we ordinarily think of schools, though not quite consciously, as the "culture" itself, little models of society. We try to fit the student into the model, believing that if he will adjust to it he will in some way have been "civilized." That

111

approach is connected to the needs of the early century, when the schools were the means by which the children of immigrant parents were acculturated and moved from the European values of their parents toward more prevalent American ones. But all of that has changed now. The children in our schools, all of them, are little fragments of *this* culture; they no longer need to be "socialized" in the same ways. The specific experiences of every adolescent—his fears, his family crises, his dreams and hallucinations, his habits, his sexuality—all these are points at which the general culture reveals itself in some way. There is no longer any real question of getting the adolescent to "adjust" to things.

The problem is a different one: What kind of setting will enable him to discover and accept what is already within him; to articulate it and perceive the extent to which it is shared with others; and, finally, to learn to change it within and outside himself? For that is what I mean when I call the adolescent a "maker of value." He is a trustee, a trustee of a world that already exists in some form within himself—and we must both learn, the adolescent and his teachers, to respect it.

In a sense, then, I am calling for a reversal of most educational thought. The individual is central; the individual, in the deepest sense, *is* the culture, not the institution. His culture resides in him, in experience and memory, and what is needed is an education that has at its base the sanctity of the individual's experience and leaves it intact.

What keeps running through my mind is a line I read twelve years ago in a friend's first published story: *The Idea in that idea is: there is no one over you.* I like that line: *There is no one over you.* Perhaps that signifies the gap between these children and their parents. For the children it is true, they sense it: there is no one over them; believable authority has disappeared; it has been replaced by experience. As Thomas Altizer says, God is dead; he is experienced now not as someone above or omnipotent or omniscient or "outside," but inwardly, as conscience or vision or even the unconscious or Tillich's "ground of being." This is all too familiar to bother with here, but this particular generation is a collective dividing point. The parents of these children, the fathers, still believe in "someone" over them, insist upon it; in fact, demand it for and from their children. The children themselves cannot believe it; the idea means nothing to them. It is almost as if they are the first real Americans—suddenly free of Europe and somehow fatherless, confused, forced back on their own experience, their own sense of things, even though, at the same time, they are forced to defy their families and schools in order to keep it.

This is, then, a kind of Reformation. Arnold was wrong when he said that art would replace religion; education replaced it. Church became School, the principal vehicle for value, for "culture," and just as men once rebelled against the established Church as the mediator between God and man, students now rebel against the *public* school (and its version of things) as the intermediary between themselves and experience, between themselves and experience and the making of value. Students are expected to reach "reality" (whether of knowledge or society) through their teachers and school. No one, it is said, can participate in the culture effectively without having at one time passed through their hands, proven his allegiance to them, and been blessed. This is the authority exercised by priests or the Church. Just as men once moved to shorten the approach to God, they are moved now to do the same thing in relation to learning and to the community. For just as God was argued to appear within a man—unique, private, and yet shared—so culture is, in some way, grounded in the individual; it inhabits him. The schools, like the Church, must be the expression of that habitation, not its exclusive medium. This is the same reformative shift that occurred in religion, a shift from the institutional (the external) to the individual (the internal), and it demands, when it occurs, an agony, an apocalyptic frenzy, a destruction of the past itself. I believe it is happening now. One sees and feels it everywhere: a violent fissure, a kind of quake.

I remember one moment in the streets of Oakland during the draft demonstrations. The students had sealed off the street with overturned cars and there were no police; the gutters were empty and the students moved into them from the sidewalks, first walking, then running, and finally almost dancing in the street. You could almost see the idea coalesce on their faces: The street is ours! It was as if a weight had been lifted from them, a fog; there was not at that moment any fury in them, any vengefulness or even politics; rather, a lightness, delight, an exhilaration at the sudden inexplicable sense of being free. George Orwell describes something similar in *Homage to Catalonia*: that brief period in Barcelona when the anarchists had apparently succeeded and men shared what power there was. I don't know how to describe it, except to say that one's inexplicable sense of invisible authority had vanished: the oppressive father, who is not really there, was gone.

That sudden feeling is familiar to us all. We have

all had it from time to time in our own lives, that sense of "being at home," that ease, that feeling of a Paradise which is neither behind us nor deferred but is around us, a natural household. It is the hint and beginning of Manhood: a promise, a clue. One's attention turns to the immediate landscape and to one's fellows: toward what is there, toward what can be felt as a part of oneself. I have seen the same thing as I watched Stokely Carmichael speaking to a black audience and telling them that they must stop begging the white man, like children, for their rights. They were, he said, neither children nor slaves, no, they were—and here they chanted, almost cried, in unison —a beautiful people: *yes our noses are broad and our lips are thick and our hair is kinky . . . but we are beautiful, we are beautiful, we are black and beautiful.* Watching, you could sense in that released joy an emergence, a surfacing of pride, a refusal to accept shame or the white man's dominance—and a turning to one another, to their own inherent value.

But there is a kind of pain in being white and watching that, for there is no one to say the same things to white children; no "fathers" or brothers to give them that sense of manhood or pride. The adolescents I have seen—white, middle-class—are a long way from those words *we are beautiful, we are beautiful.* I cannot imagine how they will reach them, deprived as they are of all individual strength. For the schools exist to deprive one of strength. That is why one's own worth must be proven again and again by the satisfaction of external requirements with no inherent value or importance; it is why one must satisfy a set of inexplicable demands; it is why there is a continual separation of self and worth and the intrusion of a kind of institutional guilt: failure not of God but of *the system,* the nameless "others," the authority that one can never quite see; and it explains the oppressive sense of some nameless transgression, almost a shame at Being itself.

It is this feeling that pervades both high schools and college, this Kafkaesque sense of faceless authority that drives one to rebellion or withdrawal, and we are all, for that reason, enchanted by the idea of the Trial, that ancient Socratic dream of confrontation and vindication or martyrdom. It is then, of course, that Authority shows its face. In the mid-fifties I once watched Jack Kerouac on a television show and when the interviewer asked him what he wanted he said: to see the face of God. How arrogant and childish and direct! And yet, I suppose, it is what we all want as children: to have the masks of authority, all its disguises, removed and to see it plain. That is what lies in large part behind the riots in the schools. Their specific grievances are incidental; their real purpose is to make God show his face, to have whatever pervasive and oppressive force makes us perpetual children reveal itself, declare itself, commit itself at last. It is Biblical; it is Freudian; it reminds me in some way of the initiation rites: the need to unmask the gods and assume their power, to become an equal—and to find in that the manhood one has been denied.

The schools seem to enforce the idea that there *is* someone over you; and the methods by which they do it are ritualized, pervasive. The intrusion of guilt, shame, alienation from oneself, dependence, insecurity—all these feelings are not the accidental results of schools; they are intentional, and they are used in an attempt to make children manipulable, obedient, "good citizens" we call it, and useful to the state. The schools are the means by which we deprive the young of manhood—that is what I mean to say—

and we must not be surprised when they seek that manhood in ways that must of necessity be childish and violent.

℣

But I must admit this troubles me, for there is little choice between mindless violence and mindless authority, and I am just enough of an academic, an intellectual, to want to preserve much of what will be lost in the kind of rebellion or apocalypse that is approaching. And yet, and yet . . . the rapidity of events leaves me with no clear idea, no solution, no sense of what will be an adequate change. It may be that all of this chaos is a way of breaking with the old world and that from it some kind of native American will emerge. There is no way of knowing, there no longer seems any way of estimating what is necessary or what will work. I know only that the problem now seems to be that our response to crisis is to move away or back rather than forward, and that we will surely, for the sake of some imagined order, increase in number and pressure the very approaches that have brought us to this confusion. I don't know. I believe that the young must have values, of course, be responsible, care, but I know too that most of the violence I have seen done to the young has been done in the name of value, and that the well-meaning people who have been so dead set on making things right have had a hand in bringing us to where we are now. The paradox is a deep and troubling one for me. I no longer know if change can be accomplished—for the young, for any of us, without the apocalyptic fury that seems almost upon us. The crisis of youth and education is symptomatic of some larger, deeper fault in our cities and minds, and perhaps nothing can be done consciously in those areas until the air itself is violently cleared one way or another.

So I have no easy conclusions, no startling synthesis with which to close. I have only a change in mood, a softening, a kind of sadness. It may be, given that, that the best thing is simply to close with an unfinished fragment in which I catch for myself the hint of an alternative:

. . . I am trying to surround you, I see that, I am trying to make with these words a kind of city so natural, so familiar, that the other world, the one that appears to be, will look by comparison absurd and flat, limited, unnecessary. What I am after is liberation, not my own, which comes often enough these days in solitude or sex, but yours, and that is arrogant, isn't it, that is presumptuous, and yet that is the function of art: to set you free. It is that too which is the end of education: a liberation from childhood and what holds us there, a kind of midwifery, as if the nation itself were in labor and one wanted to save both the future and the past—for we are both, we are, we are the thin bridge swaying between them, and to tear one from the other means a tearing of ourselves, a partial death.

And yet it may be that death is inevitable, useful. It may be. Perhaps, as in the myth, Aphrodite can rise only where Cronos' testicles have fallen into the sea. It may be that way with us. The death of the Father who is in us, the death of the old authority which is part of us, the death of the past which is also our death; it may all be necessary: a rending and purgation. And yet one still seeks another way, somethings less (or is it more) apocalyptic, a way in which the past becomes the future in ourselves, in which we become the bridges between: makers of culture.

Unless from us the future takes place, we are Death

only, *said Lawrence, meaning what the Chassids do: that the world and time reside within, not outside, men; that there is no distance, no "alienation," only a perpetual wedding to the world. It is that—the presence in oneself of Time—that makes things interesting, is more gravid and interesting than guilt. I don't want to lose it, don't want to relinquish that sense in the body of another dimension, a distance, the depth of the body as it extends backward into the past and forward, as it contains and extends and transforms.*

What I am after is an alternative to separation and rage, some kind of connection to things to replace the system of dependence and submission—the loss of the self—that now holds sway, slanted toward violence. I am trying to articulate a way of seeing, of feeling, that will restore to the young a sense of manhood and potency without at the same time destroying the past. That same theme runs through whatever I write: the necessity for each man to experience himself as an extension and maker of culture, and to feel the whole force of the world within himself, not as an enemy—but as himself:

. . . An act of learning is a meeting, and every meeting is simply the discovery in the world of a part of oneself that had previously been unacknowledged by the self. It is the recovery of the extent of one's being. It is the embrace of an eternal but elusive companion, the shadowy "other" in which one truly resides and which blazes, when embraced, like the sun. ❧

Permanence and Change

ROBERT M. HUTCHINS

My text is taken from the words of John Dewey in his essay "My Pedagogic Creed." He said: "The only possible adjustment which we can give to the child under existing conditions is that which arises through putting him in complete possession of all his powers. With the advent of democracy and modern industrial conditions, it is impossible to foretell definitely just what civilization will be twenty years from now. Hence it is impossible to prepare the child for any precise set of conditions."

These words were written in 1897. As we look back over the last seventy years and reflect on the changes that have taken place since Dewey wrote, we see that he did not exaggerate. If he were living today, he would feel compelled, I think, to shorten the time interval he mentions. Twenty years is now an eternity.

At a recent meeting of the research committee of the California Commission on Manpower, Automation, and Technology, the man in charge of the training of vocational teachers in the state asked the industrialists present to give him some indication of what vocational education teachers would need to know seven years from now. He was greeted with incredulous laughter. The man from Lockheed said he could not say what kind of training his workers would need seven months from now.

The most obvious fact about education is the one most often overlooked: it takes time.

The most obvious fact about society is that the more technological it is the more rapidly it will change. It follows that in an advanced technological society futility dogs the footsteps of those who try to prepare the child for any precise set of conditions. Hence the most impractical education is the one that looks most practical, and the one that is most practical in fact is the one that is commonly regarded as remote from reality, one dedicated to the comprehension of theory and principles.

In the present state of technology, and even more certainly in any future state thereof, the kind of training and information that is central in American education is obsolescent, if not obsolete. Now, the only possible adjustment that we can give the child is that which arises through putting him in complete possession of all his powers.

From a curriculum aiming to make the schools contribute to this result neither training nor information would disappear. But they would be different. The training would be in techniques the child would need under any conditions, in any occupation, at any stage of his life. Such techniques are language and mathematics, which are implicated in everything we do. The information would be such as to confirm, refute, or illustrate the principles under discussion.

If we follow Dewey's prescription, we shall try to get the child ready for anything: if we try to get him ready for something, it may not be there when we have got him ready. About all we can say today is that the one certain calling is citizenship and the one certain destiny, manhood. No occupation—perhaps not even teaching—is immune from technological change. The antibiotics have made the expensively acquired techniques of surgery in certain fields, like mastoiditis, unnecessary. A glance at an automated bakery will convince you that the managing director of Bahlsen's in Germany was right when he said, "Here the skill of the baker dies."

On the other hand, we can never have too many wise citizens or good men. The future of civilization depends on our having a more adequate supply of both. I suggest that the way to get it may be to put all children in complete possession of all their powers.

I repeat "all" children. Admittedly, the effort will carry us beyond the field for which educational administrators are responsible. In the first place, the school cannot do the whole job. Other institutions and agencies have their role. The specific function of education is to help people to become human by helping them learn to use their minds. In the second place, we have good reason to believe now that the environment, particularly the environment of the earliest years, before the child goes to school, decisively affects his performance in school.

The Coleman Report even intimates that all the factors determining a child's success or failure in school are beyond the control of that institution. The Newsom Report, in England, dealing with children of "average or less than average ability," offers evidence in the same direction.

It says of one place it studied, "the children live in back-to-back houses . . . and have no indoor sanitation—four or five families share one public toilet in the middle of the yard. Few of the children here have even seen a bathroom, and in some houses there is not even a towel and soap. All these homes have overcrowded living and sleeping quarters; for example, ten or eleven people may sleep in two beds and one cot. The girls accept drunkenness as part of the normal pattern. Twenty-two per cent of the children in one school have no father, five per cent no mother."

These children are reported to have average or less than average ability. It is amazing they have any ability at all. For what do we mean by ability in school? We mean the ability to compete on even terms in matters literary and intellectual with children from homes in which there are conversation, books, and some sense of the value of education—to say nothing of bathrooms.

All educational standards, no matter how "scientific," are culturally derived. The celebrated Intelligence Quotient, the I.Q., must favor the child who has been fortunate in his early surroundings against one who has lived in the English or American slums. With the best buildings, a permanent staff of the best teachers, and an inspiring curriculum, what hope is there unless the cause of the difficulty, the slum itself, is eliminated? And what can the schools do about that?

René Dubos believes that as much as eighty per cent of the genetic potential of most human beings may be repressed by their environment. Neither he nor anybody else would claim that the genetic potential of all human beings is the same; but we can all agree that the child's potential, whatever it is, should, as far as possible, be protected from environmental obliteration.

It used to be assumed that there were different kinds of people, those who could be educated and those who could not be. We know now that man makes himself by making the environment in which he places the newborn. Where racial discrimination inhibits mobility, where poverty suppresses human possibilities, it will be difficult to put any child in complete possession of all his powers.

Boarding schools, whose quality of education we

must now give all children, have been the privilege of the rich. The education designed to put the child in complete possession of his highest powers has, in effect, been limited to those from what are called "good homes." The others, who have confronted an alien culture when they came to school, have been shunted off into vocational training, lower tracks, or the labor market. They have been thought of as ineducable.

As long as they live under adverse circumstances they will not be able to cope with a school that was not built for them. But as Jensen's work at Berkeley shows, their learning ability may be high and, if we spend the money, time, and care necessary to develop it, many of them can conquer the obstacles that have been fatal to their educational careers.

There can be no question that the tracking system as it is employed today in mixed schools of Negroes and whites is a means of perpetuating poverty and racial discrimination. This is not because of ill will or because of any conspiracy. I am confident that in the overwhelming majority of cases children are properly placed in the proper tracks on the basis of adequate tests. I am attacking not the administration of the tracking system, but the system itself. A big rescue job has to be done with pupils who come from the suffocating atmosphere of our slums and ghettos. The first step in rescuing them is to signify to them and everybody else in the school that they are not inferior and that they will receive no fewer educational opportunities than their contemporaries.

Segregation on the basis of color is worse than segregation on the basis of "ability." The ghetto schools have to be improved. Such improvement, to the extent that it is possible, should not be used to justify our failure to break up the ghettos. Open-housing legislation could have a more important influence on education than any educational innovations in the ghetto schools.

We have to abolish the ghettos and slums. Meanwhile, we have to improve the schools that are there. Both these operations will require vast sums of money. I do not need to point out where the money could come from. I need only say that in my judgment thirty billion dollars a year is available, some part of which could be used for the education of our people and for the assistance of the rest of mankind.

An automated society can be a learning society, one in which the object of the community is, as John Stuart Mill suggested, the virtue and intelligence of the people. The question is, what are we going to learn? If we follow John Dewey, we shall hope to put the child in complete possession of his intellectual power, and we shall expect him as he grows up and goes on through adult life to continue the development of that power. This will obviously not be for the purpose of earning a living. The aim must be to become a complete human being, a wise citizen, and a good man, living, as Ortega used to say, "at the height of his times." I do not underestimate training or the acquisition of technical competence. I merely say that where technical competence is required it will, in view of the rapidity of change, have to be gained on the job. On the same job, retraining may have to occur very often. But what we are trying to find out is not how those who need them may learn techniques but how to put all Americans in complete possession of all their powers.

What we are looking for is a new definition of

liberal education. We need a definition of it appropriate to the world we are now entering, one characterized by very rapid change, by vast stretches of free time, by the emergence of a world order, and by the urgent demand for wise citizens and good men. We have to make the effort to help everybody achieve this education. The proportions of this effort are indicated by the unanimity with which liberal education has been thought of as the privilege of the few. When what are called "the masses" began to enter the education system, liberal education had to be diluted to the point of insipidity. It is almost non-existent in this country today. So-called colleges of liberal arts, in which only the name survives, announce that the student is liberally educated when he has accumulated 120 semester hours of miscellaneous credits in his academic account book. As things are today, more than half these credits, and the ones that really count, are those obtained in courses aiming at technical competence in some vocational field.

In the rest of the world liberal education appears to be in retreat, and for the strangest of reasons. The reason is that education is everywhere coming to be recognized as a universal human right. Therefore, everybody is entitled to it. But nobody, so the argument goes, is entitled to any better education than anybody else. Since the great majority of the population is alleged to be too stupid to profit by liberal education, the minority that could profit by it must be deprived of it. These notions have transformed the slogan, education for all, into the idea of inferior education for all. On this point see the current discussion in England in which the Left proposes, instead of extending the benefits of elite "public school" education to everybody, abolishing this kind of education altogether.

No doubt the institutions dedicated to liberal education here and elsewhere were started as elite schools. At a time when every European had a station in life, that to which his parents belonged, and when he was educated, if at all, for that station, it was natural that these institutions, which were designed for the future rulers of the commonwealth, should be limited to the children of the upper classes.

These schools made no pretense of being democratic. They developed a technology of education suited to the background of the pupils they admitted. Pupils with other backgrounds, if they could summon up the courage to scale the battlements of these institutions, found themselves facing an alien culture and a pedagogy designed for that culture. In the ordinary case, they did not try to enter, and when they did enter, they failed.

The remnants of this tradition are scattered all over the place. Socio-economic status, everywhere in the world, determines the length of one's formal education and one's success in it. So when we talk about liberal education today we are plagued by reminiscences and overtones of elitism, aristocracy, and snobbery. It is assumed that something insidiously undemocratic is afoot. But I suggest that true democrats are those who believe that everybody must be educated for freedom, and anti-democrats are those who think there are two kinds of people, those who can be educated and those who can be trained, those who can become human beings and those who are, in Aristotle's phrase, "natural slaves."

The only education worth having in an age of rapid change is liberal education. The formulation of it that we have to discover must meet certain requirements. It must be for all. It must lay the foundations for wise citizenship, the sensible use of leisure, and the continuous development of the highest powers of every human being. It must be the kind of education that will bind men together, not merely in this country but throughout the world; for a world order is emerging.

Harvey Wheeler has said, "In unconsciously creating a unitary industrial world order, man has made his survival depend upon his ability to follow it by a consciously created political order. . . . *Homo sapiens* is everywhere the same. . . . The forces of science, technology, urbanization, industrial development, the mass media, and world integration carry the same imperatives wherever they reach."

An education that tried to assist the formation of the world community would seek to connect rather than divide men; it would seek to do so by drawing out the elements of their common humanity. It would be theoretical rather than practical, because, though men do different things, they can all share in understanding. It would be general rather than specialized, because, though all men are not experts in the same subject, they all ought to grasp the same principles. It would be liberal rather than vocational, because, though all men do not follow the same occupations, the minds of all men should be set free. An education that helps all men to become human by helping them gain complete possession of all their powers would seem to be the only defensible education in a world of rapid technological change; it would seem to be the best for a national community and for the world community as well.

There are no longer any national problems. Or, to put it another way, all national problems are world problems. The United States cannot be an island of power and prosperity in a world of weakness and squalor. That ought to be clear by now. It is equally evident that the United States needs an education that aims not at its own power and prosperity but at the development of the humanity of all mankind. This means dedication to liberal education at home and abroad. The rapidity of technological change, which requires us to take liberal education for all seriously, is a worldwide phenomenon that requires us to take liberal education seriously on a global scale.

We hear a great deal today about relevance and involvement. Education is supposed to be relevant to contemporary issues, and this relevance, it is often suggested, is to be obtained through involvement in action that, it is hoped, will affect contemporary events. I strongly favor relevance and involvement in this sense of these words on one condition, and that is that we recall that education takes time and that we live in a world of very rapid change. Contemporary events and involvement in them are of the first importance if the object is to understand them and through understanding them to refine the principles by which they are understood. However, a curriculum composed only of current events and involvement in them cannot be educational, because by definition current events do not stay current.

I should like to say a word on behalf of critical distance. We see its value easily enough in the matter of language. A child breathes in his mother tongue. He does not understand it, because he does not have to. It is probably fair to say that he never will understand it unless he studies another language. Then he is likely to see for the first time that his own has a comprehensible structure. In the same way, we breathe in the American Way of Life. We assume it is the only way to live because we do not understand it, because we do not understand other ways of life, and because to suggest that the American way could be improved is often regarded as "unpatriotic." But if America is to discharge her responsibilities in a rapidly changing world her citizens have got to be able to appraise her ideals and her performance in terms of standards that can command the respect of mankind. This will involve the effort to discover and comprehend those standards.

This permits me to say a word on behalf of tradition, by which I understand the transmission of our cultural heritage. This is clearly something more than the American way of life. It is the accumulated wisdom of the race. In a rapidly changing world we can recognize it by applying a pragmatic test: it is those works of the mind which illuminate or are likely to illuminate human life under any conditions that may arise.

One way to achieve critical distance is to achieve knowledge of the tradition. If we cannot be sure where we are going, we can at least find out where we have been; we can discover in the reflections of our greatest predecessors suggestions about where we might go and what the advantages or disadvantages of going one way or another may be, and we can try to exert ourselves as intelligently and resolutely as possible in the direction indicated by rational inquiry and debate.

The aim of American education in an age of rapid change should be to do what it can to help everybody gain complete possession of all his powers. As John Dewey says, this is the only possible aim. It is now clear that the only thing we can do is what we ought to have been doing all along. ❧

Bringing Science Under Law

HARVEY WHEELER

In referring to science and technology here, I am invoking the distinction Linus Pauling once made between "developmental" science and what is usually called "pure" science. By developmental science Pauling did not mean merely technology nor did he mean only bureaucratized science, i.e. the mass coöperative endeavor that takes place in great institutes and business corporations. Rather, he had in mind the day-to-day work of the brilliant men who are exploring the implications of the breakthroughs made by first-magnitude geniuses.

One distinctive feature of developmental science is its rapid technological transformation. In fact, the pace of technological application is such that developmental science these days is almost immediately converted into technology. In speaking of science in this article, I have this in mind. I am not, in a word, concerned with the basement-and-garret science of the lonely pioneering genius. — H. W.

A shock reverberated through the intellectual establishment of the West in the mid-twentieth century when it became apparent that science was not necessarily incompatible with totalitarianism. The West had previously "proved" on paper that science required the so-called free market in ideas, a John Stuart Mill type of liberal democracy, in order to flourish. This, it now became clear, was simply not true.

There had been an even more disturbing revelation earlier. Nazi Germany had shown that even the most "ethical" of the professions, medicine, was capable of turning its humanitarian code into a license to perform gruesome experiments on living people. While this was chilling, it also seemed at the time to be too perverse to be a threat elsewhere. Now, however, with authoritarianism increasing throughout the West, and with organ transplants becoming commonplace, we are beginning to have vague fears that something similar to the Nazi corruption of medical science might be looming for all of us.

A third shock occurred after World War II when we learned that our own American scientists had eagerly produced history's most awesome weapons, hardly stopping to consider that moral issues might be involved in their decision to do so. Science, these eminent men insisted, was ethically neutral.

Recently, a technological development renewed our concern. Dramatic developments in mathematical logic, cybernation, systems analysis, and the planning-programming-budgeting approach to administrative control have been giving us reason of late to believe that a science-spawned managerial revolution may yet be in the offing. During the past twenty years or so, it has begun to appear that management may gain access to techniques and tools that could be used to achieve their managerial ends without concern for the public good.

The appearance of a new technology, of course,

need not necessarily be a matter of concern unless another factor is present; that is, the new technology and its practitioners must be engaged in doing something that intimately affects the public interest. When this happens there are grave potentials for harming, as well as benefiting, society. The question, then, arises as to whether or not we can or should act collectively to inhibit the harmful effects that may result from the bad uses of science and technology. This is our present problem.

Currently many solutions are being offered. One is to find some way of revivifying the classical idea of the profession. Another is to create some sort of government agency charged with coördinating science policy. Both solutions strike me as seriously deficient. Nothing less than an entirely new look at science will suffice. This requires discussion of what has come to be known as the scientific revolution.

The process by which the A-bomb was created pointed up the inner political logic of that revolution. It also laid bare the corrosive impact developmental science is having on our traditional liberal democratic dogmas and practices. The birth of the bomb demonstrated once and for all that neither the people, their elected representatives, nor even bureaucratic experts are competent any longer to "legislate" about scientific problems. The traditional deliberative processes of Western democracy, it is clear, were undermined when it became apparent that they could not cope with the implications of contemporary science for public policy.

But there was also a positive side. The implications of the new science ranged far beyond the interests and activities of the scientific establishment itself; fundamental scientific innovations, such as those relating to atomic energy and solid-state physics, furnished the foundations on which the very shape of society would be built in the future. Important scientific discoveries had always brought about profound social changes, of course. But as long as these discoveries occurred infrequently and without conscious anticipation, much less design, one could not say that they were called forth politically. However, with the maturity of the sciences, Francis Bacon's *New Atlantis* became a prescription for the present rather than a fanciful vision of the future. The time, then, had arrived when science made it possible to "legislate" the shape of the future.

This shifted politics to a new plane. Those who had produced the atom bomb were actually the first to see that they had wrought not only a scientific but a political revolution — legislatures might continue to operate in their accustomed fashion, politicians might continue to campaign for office as of old, but those who were really determining the outlines of the future belonged to the scientific, rather than the political, establishment. As a consequence of these developments, the significance of today's scientific revolution can be summarized simply: The revolution has brought about social transformations; relationships between theory and practice that seemingly had been firmly established by the Industrial Revolution were reversed. This change means, among other things, that in the world created by the scientific revolution the critical force in society will no longer be the flow of capital but scientific and technological innovation. The most fateful struggles in that society will be fought over the efforts to direct and control these innovations. This is where constitutionalization comes in.

Our notion of legislation and/or constitutionalization has long been built on two assumptions, neither of which is now acceptable. The first was that men of common prudence and wisdom are capable of understanding every political problem that needs to be understood. The second was that such men could make laws to deal with these problems. The scientific revolution is undermining the first of these assumptions by posing problems too technical for laymen to fathom. It is undermining the second by making it impossible for legislatures to lay the foundation for the future. The result is already evident; we either have to invent new procedures for handling science policy or be ruled by technology.

How do we deal with the problem? At first blush, it might seem enough merely to strengthen our governing institutions with more scientific advisers. But this is not enough; it won't do. The reason is that the scientific expert has to be such a narrow specialist he cannot acquire the general knowledge necessary to grasp the social and philosophical implications of even those technical matters on which he is an acknowledged expert. The same thing applies in reverse. The generalist's knowledge of any one specialty is not thorough enough for him to master the complex problems now associated with science and technology.

There is a philosophical issue here. It turns on a very old argument about science — one as old as the temptation of Adam and Eve, the curiosity of Pandora, or Prometheus' defiance of the gods. Perhaps of all such myths, the Doctor Faustus story is the most pertinent.

That myth embodied the essential ethic of medieval science — something the men of the Middle Ages took very seriously. Remember they did not look upon science as ineffectual. On the contrary, everyone believed in its power — black magic it was called — just as everyone believed in white magic, the power of miracles. But one magic was satanic and the other godly. One defied God and incurred His wrathful retribution; the other entailed His bountiful intervention.

The war between the two varieties of magic was carried over into attacks on magicians who practiced the black arts of alchemy and astrology and employed spells, secret words, cabalistic designs, talismanic charms, and amulets to gain power over the spirits who — it was widely believed — were in control of human events. As the various departments of magic matured into the post-medieval sciences, the pioneers were anxious to purge science of this reliance on supernatural forces. At the same time they were eager to proclaim their own religious orthodoxy. Such, at least, was the aim of Copernicus, Galileo, Brahe, and Vesalius. It was also the later concern of Descartes, Bacon, Newton, and Leibnitz. But, though science was changing the face of the earth, the theologians still looked at the world in the old manner. As a result, the old war between black and white magic turned into a new war between science and religion.

The leading early apologist for the new view of science was Francis Bacon. Bacon claimed that science had no theological significance; like heaven and earth, theology and science were simply different realms of truth. To make his case, Bacon and his followers invoked the Biblical text that distinguished between the things owing to Caesar and those owing to God. They argued from it that a man could be faithful to one and yet serve the other. Beyond this, Bacon held that there was something intrinsically humanistic about science. It advanced human knowledge, which in turn contributed to human progress. The only thing necessary, then, was to keep science free of dogma and authority.

Bacon's position in time became the professional ideology of science, to such an extent that it seemed to be a self-evident truth. All seemed to be going well — the ideology went largely unchallenged — until the contemporary scientific revolution reopened certain ethical issues that had remained closed since the seventeenth century. We are, in a sense, then, back to Doctor Faustus.

Recall that the Faustian legend was informed with a view that had science dependent on the special intervention of supernatural forces. Medieval science had sought for ultimate power and knowledge — omnipotence and omniscience, the attributes of God. The scientists of that period, in a word, had pursued the most fundamental quests. They tried to plumb directly to the secrets of the creation of life. They sought the magical elixir that would bring everlasting youth, searched for the philosopher's stone that would convert the baser metals into the finer, puzzled over the secret "signatures" of events that would unlock the mysteries of past and future and produce control over the paths of the planets and the vagaries of the weather. They propitiated spirits who could empower them to move mountains, change men into different shapes, and permit moving about through space and time at will. With such goals, the prospects for science were more revolutionary, and the risks incurred by its practitioners far more dangerous, than what was to come later. Medieval science, then, faced up to the questions about men who would play God. The advent of the early-modern sciences required a new informal "contract" in place of the older one Faustus had negotiated with Satan. According to the new pact, scientists would abandon all the quests that were disturbing to theologians in return for freedom to work without interference. As scientists they would stay out of God's province, concerning themselves only with the problems of this world. Theologians and philosophers for their part would stop pillorying science. Francis Bacon drafted this "contract" for the Anglo-Saxon world; it was also described by Descartes and Leibnitz.

Although modern science abandoned an over-all ethic, it did adopt a kind of internal code. The scientist was supposed to maintain his methodological and intellectual honesty, but that was all. Hence, from a deeper standpoint, early-modern science was ethically barren, and proud of it. This, however, will no longer do. Science today is once more delving into something like the quests pursued by medieval magic. For example, the deliberate synthesis of miracle fabrics, exotic metals, and precious stones has become an everyday occurrence. The genetic code through which the rudimentary substances of life are ordered into their distinctive shapes and functions has been deciphered. The French physicist Pierre Auger has even suggested that molecular biologists may succeed in recalling previously extinct animal forms from the burial grounds of history. The contemporary scientist must, then, face the ethical problem Doctor Faustus confronted. Unfettered freedom for developmental science is no longer tolerable. Scientists themselves recognize it, as was evident in the bad consciences of some of those who built the atom bomb.

The distinguished physicist Max Born has pointed to a source for the ethical corrosion in modern science. For men to be ethical they must perceive the moral implications of the alternative actions open to them. This is not necessarily a pragmatic or utilitarian view of ethics, for even if one holds that such things as murder are evil the hard question comes when we have to decide in a given case exactly what constitutes "murder" and whether or not there are circumstances that might justify it. Ordinarily, ethical judgments of this kind are not too difficult. If a military commander orders a subordinate to commit a crime against humanity, the soldier may decide he has no alternative but to obey. However, he cannot claim ignorance of the ethical issue. The case of the scientist, though, is somewhat different. When a scientist sets out to produce atomic bombs or death rays, the preliminary research may be on such an abstract level that the connection between pure science and the purpose for the research effectively disappears. The scientists working on such projects can dispel any ethical qualms they might have by intoning the traditional ideology: any augmentation of knowledge must be good. In short, ethical judgments require making a connection between actions and effects, and it is this connection that science dissolves. Moreover, the full implications of a scientific discovery may not become completely apparent for many years. A scientist may work in full innocence only to learn years later that he helped produce a horror.

It has always been true, of course, that an action in the present may have unforeseeable harmful effects in the distant future. The invention of the automobile is an all too familiar illustration. A similar separation — not in time but in function — accompanies bureaucratization. Bureaucracy transforms people into impersonal functionaries. This was one reason Nazi concentration-camp executives could go about their duties seemingly detached from the atrocities they administered. A similar effect occurs when science becomes bureaucratized — the individual scientist deals with so minute a segment of the over-all project that he becomes almost as detached from the implications of his work as Adolf Eichmann alleged he was. Now contemporary science is raising this separation between actions and their effects to a new level. The more profound a scientific innovation, the more universal its potential applications — and the more difficult it becomes to foresee its extended effects. Professor Born's mournful conclusion was that the contemporary scientific revolution has destroyed ethics, ushering mankind into a new world that is not only post-industrial but post-ethical.

Ethics is philosophical but practical; science is logical and mathematical in form. The result is that scientific knowledge accumulates from generation to generation like the compound interest on savings deposits. Each new scientist stands on the shoulders of those who have gone before, leaving behind him a hundred more who will do the same in turn. Each fledgling scientist begins his career by mastering the distilled essences of the work of his predecessors, his lifetime is devoted to adding elements to the accumulated scientific edifice. He need not, indeed, start out by retracing all the laborious steps that have brought science from its earliest beginnings to its present elevated state. If that were necessary, the progress of science would be limited to how much of it could be assimilated anew by each successive neophyte: science could not develop beyond the limits of scientific powers one man could bring to bear in the course of a single lifetime.

This latter condition, however, was roughly the case before the advent of modern science. Prior to that, the quest for both scientific and ethical knowledge proceeded in much the same way. Both were subject to similar limitations and neither could systematically develop and accumulate its findings. Bacon, realizing this, was right in seizing upon augmentation as the trademark of early-modern science.

When, in the seventeenth century, science acquired this power of augmentation, the growth of scientific knowledge shot up at an exponential rate, while ethical knowledge remained, and remains to this day, much as before. The social effect of such knowledge — that is, its capacity for good — is limited by the amount of wisdom individual men can acquire during their lifetime, for one does not assimilate the truth of an ethical precept the way one grasps the truth of a mathematical solution. On the contrary, one must first become a philosopher to perceive the validity of the teachings of the wise men who have gone before. Coué was wrong, with his doctrine that every day in every way we are getting better and better. His error, and that of the doctrine of progress, was in assuming that the augmentation observable in the sciences was applicable to moral philosophy. On the contrary, moral philosophy has progressed but little during its entire twenty-five hundred years of history.

Each man must learn and apply ethical truths for himself. This is an additional basis for the contemporary separation between science and ethics. As science progresses cumulatively the problems it poses become progressively more numerous and complex. The gap between science and ethics widens with each passing hour. Some relief might develop were science able to extend human longevity, permitting us to devote more time to the quest for wisdom. Short of this, however, the only solution would appear to lie in a concerted effort to constitutionalize science, so that its progress and development can be subjected to planning and control. A new ethic of science must be developed. We face a genuine culture crisis. This would be true even if, improbably, science were to grind to a halt and technological developments based on it were to cease. If today's life scientists are correct, the present crisis will shortly take an even more ominous turn.

The life sciences — biology, genetics, and so forth — are on the brink of a revolutionary development that will usurp the primacy that the physical sciences have enjoyed for over three hundred years. But note one difference: tampering with life processes demands ethical norms. Sciences that deal with life processes cannot avoid questions concerned with the goals, ends, and purposes of life. The tragedy, however, is that such questions do not interest most scientists, while philosophers by and large are not interested in what science is doing. Nonetheless, anything connected with the life processes involves ethics. It is *there,* unavoidable, lying at the heart of the life sciences. Yet, the biological sciences matured under the hegemony of the physical sciences — and, more's the pity, their recent spectacular advances have come from molecular biology, whose operating assumption is that life processes can be reduced to the principles of physics. The life sciences, then, have reached maturity with the amoral pursuit of "objectivity" that long characterized the physical sciences. Inasmuch as life is intrinsically normative, the contemporary ethical poverty of biology must be due to some more fundamental development that made this distortion seem plausible. I suggest it was the ancient maneuver whereby all nature, life as well as inert matter, was made profane. The maneuver predated modern science by nearly sixteen hundred years. It can be traced back to that point in the Western tradition when both nature and society were secularized. The striking fact is that not science but Christianity turns out to be the culprit.

Prior to the advent of Christianity there had been no secular society and there had been no secular view of nature in Western tradition. On the contrary, as with practically every other known culture, society and nature were regarded as intrinsically sacral. This, of course, was the point at issue between the early Christians and the ancient Romans. The Christians' way of stating this was that the one true God forbade their participation in the rituals of any other god. Viewed in the light of today's enlarged perspective, this commandment was preposterous. Worse, it smacked of the colossal effrontery of the unlettered. The urbane Romans, ironically destined to be known as pagans (peasants), pointed out that what Christians overdramatically objected to as Emperor worship was but the ritual celebration of the social order. That occurred in almost every society. Similar Roman rituals also celebrated the natural order. But the early Christians — today's Jehovah's Witnesses make much the same point — narrowly restricted the sacral to the attributes of their own remote triune God.

The issue was brought to a head four centuries later in the dramatic showdown between Saint Augustine and Bishop Faustus. Bishop Faustus represented the West's last chance to reject the hard-shell eschatology of the Christian extremists. But Augustine won that momentous battle and proceeded to establish the dualistic doctrine of the divine heavenly city and the corrupt city of this world as the official world view of the Western tradition. What Augustine wrought was, in effect, the birth of an ideology that ultimately permitted Western science to take an amoral approach to nature. In the light of the scientific revolution of our times, the Augustine-Faustus

143

debate must be revived, overturned, and an ethical view of man, society, and nature reëstablished.

❧

How would the control of developmental science, what I call constitutionalization, work? Perhaps the A.E.C., Telstar, and the T.V.A. can serve as examples. A public corporation for developmental science can be chartered and given its constitution. Civilian control can be installed and charged with the responsibility for several functions that are now not being performed at all. Most obvious is the need for an ombudsman to process public complaints as well as complaints from scientists inside the Establishment. The ombudsman should have positive, as well as negative, or corrective, functions. That is, in addition to investigating alleged evils he should also see that the scientific enterprise achieves its publicly approved goals. This would require a special court system of adjudication, complete with appeal procedures.

To approach science in this way requires a new conception of constitutional theory — an architectonic approach to the politics of science. In such a framework, intellectual endeavors would be thought of in broad political terms, rather than merely in terms of the narrow desires of those who wish to pursue knowledge for its own, or their own, sake. It would also require fresh thought about problems such as representation, which we thought the eighteenth century had put to rest for all times. If there is to be a new kind of public corporation for science, if it is to be under civilian control, and if the public will is to make its voice heard, then there must be some way for that will to find expression. This raises the "legislative" question of how to furnish science with responsible policy-forming and goal-establishing functions. We know that the scandalous scientific boondoggling of the recent past must be prevented. Scientists themselves have publicized certain unsavory aspects of "big science" — the space program and the Mohole project are examples. In addition to the fact that science may harm us, scientists sometimes make incredibly bad judgments about the conduct of their own affairs. Hence, science must be provided with a specially designed legislature, and, for civilian control to work, there must be participation by citizens as well as by professional scientists.

It may be that the envisioned public corporation should have a bicameral legislature, one house composed of scientists and the other of public members. One way to conceive of this would be to follow our traditional Constitutional wisdom and put financial controls and ratification powers in the public chamber and reserve the responsibility for initiating projects for the scientific chamber, with special provision for joint sessions. The proposal for a bicameral approach to science planning and policy formation immediately raises the question of a separation of powers, a checks-and-balances feature. Each house would exercise restraint on the other; concerted action would require the coöperation of both. Obviously, this new constitutionalized scientific order should not slavishly follow the established American Constitutional separation-of-powers mechanism, but certain analogues do seem promising.

This raises the question of federalism. The general Constitutional idea of federalism is "subsidiarity." It means a preference for the local over the centralized solution to problems. There may be a need in the scientific order for a special version of this principle.

This should be considered in the context of a proposed bill of rights for science. Subsidiarity dictates that every possible scientific issue be dealt with at decentralized levels, rather than being disposed of in centralized institutions. One of the chief sources of the evils we now observe in "big science" derives primarily from its centralization. Perhaps something like an anti-trust approach to science ought to be provided for. This might be the best way to protect local autonomy for our centers of scientific research.

This brings us to the necessity of educating the general public about leading scientific issues. Each sector could serve this need in its own characteristic manner. Representatives from the public sector would have to qualify for office in some way and the best way would be for them to stand for election on the basis of general programs for the development of science. Scientists, in qualifying themselves for selection by their peers, would be required to address themselves to more technical issues. Their educational role would be to uncover the extended social implications of the scientific matters at issue. A useful example was the Pauling-Teller debates a few years ago. These debates brought about a widespread public discussion of complex scientific issues. What I have proposed would regularize such public debates about the basic issues of science policy, conducted regularly by leading scientists.

There is a danger that in democratizing science we may submit it to the whims of public opinion. Many feel this would be better than leaving it to the scientists, but, of course, neither is ideal. Science is not the private property of scientists any more than the economy is the private property of businessmen, or the government the private property of politicians. Corruption occurs when scientists forget this. Actually, a scientist is much like a real-estate investor who has bought property in the path of an expanding city. When the value of his possession rises he begins to talk and act as if *he* were responsible for it. However, the individual scientist is merely the one who happens to be "in possession" at the time that knowledge is provided by massive institutional, economic, and political forces of his day. Perhaps we need a new Henry George to point out that if anybody "owns" science, it is the people themselves.

ě

In setting our own house in order, we must face the serious problem that concerns our universities and the relationships between developmental science and the proper approach to higher education. Revelations about Project Camelot and defense-oriented university research programs have made it obvious that developmental science has already distorted our educational processes and corrupted the idea of the university. The constitutional approach allows us to correct this by separating the big developmental scientific institutes and laboratories from the universities, placing them instead under public corporations.

Two things that have corrupted the sciences and professions, of course, are money and power. Whenever an endeavor becomes extremely powerful or highly profitable, its moral integrity is threatened. This would make it appear that the only people capable of maintaining an ethic for a profession are the young, before they have used it to become rich and influential. We might recall a proposition once put forward by Harold Laski. He claimed that the effective regulators of the American judiciary were the law journals, which are run by the young before they have made any money practicing law. Perhaps we can somehow institutionalize the critical and ethical talents of youth and focus them on the conduct of the sciences, as is now done for the judiciary by the law journals.

There must be some way of protecting the integrity of the scientific enterprise from corruption by either scientist or non-scientist. Traditionally such aims have been achieved through bills of rights. We are concerned here with matters such as academic freedom, the rights of students and teachers, the needs of the new Linus Paulings, the Oppenheimers, the Thorstein Veblens, and all who aspire to similar status. We are reminded once again that intellectuals are not necessarily those best qualified to understand the true needs of their own enterprise — just as businessmen are not necessarily those best qualified to understand the true needs of the economic order. Yet today's bureaucratic scientist continues to echo the nineteenth-century businessman's individualist ideology. A hundred years ago the laissez-faire ideology may have been adequate for the needs of both scientists and society. Today, however, the arguments for unhampered science are as irrelevant as the arguments for free private enterprise by mammoth corporations, or the arguments for an unregulated press by the mass-media monopolies. Three-quarters of research and development grants are for directed research. A monopoly already exists in science, and scientific freedom is largely a myth. Already, grave issues concerning intellectual freedom have arisen. Are there any projects the scientist has a right to refuse to work on? Lewis Branscom has made it clear that even if present trends continue unhampered some kind of bill of rights for science and letters will have to be instituted. The archaic ideology of science and the overweening hubris of the scientist must somehow be brought down to size. The most obvious way to do this is to provide for the constitutionalization of science in a special polity combining principles of both democracy and the rule of law. Within this context the liberties appropriate to intellectual endeavors can find proper expression and preservation.

A bill of rights reënforces the aforementioned need for a special court system. It would be necessary to provide for a prosecutor, subpoena power, and trial-like hearings. It is not possible for the common law side of our judicial system to assimilate easily these novel problems of adjudication. We will need a new jurisprudence of science, comparable to that we have developed for administrative law.

Policy formation for science means planning. It may well be that the essential nature of planning in the future will become subsumed under science policy — any other outcome would be almost inconceivable. No matter what problem we come up against — planning for the city of the future, demographic planning, resource conservation and development planning, or transportation planning — each begins from a scientific foundation and all have to be integrated into an over-all developmental program for the scientific enterprise. This requires Constitutional provision for science planning — a need that underscores the failure of our present Constitution to provide for planning of any kind. Even if science as such were to present no Constitutional issue, the need for planning should. A number of additional problems would remain even if all the innovations proposed above were to work perfectly. One of these is the relationship between the scientific and the military establishments. Three supplementary control devices may be required. One is a post-audit. This should be thought of in two ways: first, as a simple technical and financial post-audit to find out how appropriations were spent and whether irregularities occurred. But there must also be a *substantive* post-audit to inspect what actually was done in carrying out stated policies. This can be thought of as a retrospective application of planning-programming-budgeting techniques. We need to know whether space-program research and development was diverted into electronics R & D with commercial marketing potentials; whether funds for molecular biology were diverted into pharmacological research; and on down the line. Institutionalized post-audit devices are not sufficient because, as with the Army Inspector General and the federal regulatory agencies, the inspector tends to become a part of the system he inspects. Something similar to the British Commission of Inquiry is needed as well, and its quadrennial reports could coincide with the planning process and electoral campaigns. Such a commission, if staffed by men of eminence and independence, would guarantee a quality to its reports so often produced by Presidential commissions.

Another issue of major importance is the larger ecological aspect of the scientific order. What *is* this scientific order? What are its boundaries? Taken most broadly, its boundaries are those of the universe itself. This means no nation by itself can constitutionalize its own science. Suppose America had decided to develop solid-state physics and transistor applications to maximize their usefulness to the public good and avoid the dislocations too rapid exploitation brings. Similar questions concerning the computer are actually before us. It may be that intensive research on the cultural implications of the computer should be carried out before we start using it to make everything from shoes to teaching machines, flooding the consumer market with hastily conceived gadgetry. In Russia, there was insufficient hardware for immediate application when the computer first appeared. As a result, the Russians were forced, as they had been earlier in the field of rocketry, to address themselves first to the theoretical implications of the computer while they waited for the hardware to become more widely available. It may be that this simple technological lag permitted them to take a wiser view of the role of the computer than we had in this country, where it seeped through the technological order as a result of the extension of ballistics-control devices to industrial and administrative processes. But the Russian example also makes clear that no one country, not even a dictatorship, can really plan in the realm of developmental science. The history of the transistor shows that Japan, or some other country, may come along and flood the world market. Ultimately what is needed, then, is a concerted effort on a world level. It makes little difference what one nation decides to do about the transistor if any other is able to do the contrary.

So it is apparent that there is an international, or transnational, aspect to the problem of constitutionalizing science. We already have transnational industrial corporations. Perhaps the scientific order in its constitutional mode must follow the example of the transnational industrial combine. Perhaps both in unison will provide us with avenues leading toward world order. In any case, the problem of world order is here, built into contemporary developmental science. There is no way to avoid it, and we must recognize that efforts to control science must be integrated throughout the world. ⁊

The
Troubled Conscience
of the Revolutionary

DENIS GOULET

Revolutions, many argue, destroy a great deal and never actually achieve their original purposes. Even when progress results from overthrowing unjust regimes, they hold, the price is exorbitant. Consequently, they counsel patience in the face of social evils and proclaim their faith in "moderate" steps, ranging from persuasion or legislation to non-violent confrontations. From the opposite view, revolution is looked upon as a highly moral undertaking, for the champions of justice can gain the freedom necessary for radical changes in the distribution of power, wealth, and influence only if the central organs of governmental power are seized, if necessary illegally. Just as righteously as their adversaries denounce revolutionary violence, the proponents of revolution condemn the existing order as immoral, inhuman, and intolerable. Both revolutionaries and anti-revolutionaries, then, think in moral terms; yet, both are troubled, because revolutions inevitably create a dilemma for the human conscience. The alternatives — to tolerate the "intolerable" or overthrow it by force — are such that men involved in choosing between them cannot avoid evil.

When faced with a moral perplexity in the past, men were instructed by moralists to choose the lesser evil. In the case of revolution, however, this answer is useless because no one can weigh two opposite categories of evils on the same scale — the first present and unbearable, the second future and unknowable. And in the final analysis the results of revolution are always unpredictable. If history teaches anything, it is that not even the revolutionary himself knows where his acts will lead. This is why it is so tempting for students of history to conclude that there never has been a good revolution. Their argument is that the people who began revolutions never realized their original vision. Such a verdict, however, overlooks the fact that all revolutions go through a stage at which their original aims must be reconsidered, perhaps even abandoned, and new goals set in the light of lessons learned during the revolution. This happens because genuine revolution is a profound experience. The people who revolt get reëducated as well as the people against whom they are revolting. And Professor Barrington Moore reminds us that "the costs of moderation have been at least as atrocious as those of revolution, perhaps a great deal more."

As far as I can determine, every revolution has based its moral justification on its proclaimed "necessity." The reasoning is that men are sometimes so cruelly victimized by the ruling systems that to defend their humanity they simply have no moral choice but to revolt. The development in Camilo Torres' thought illustrates the point. In 1963, Torres, the revolutionary priest of Colombia, condemned violence. Three years later he wrote: "The people know that legal paths have been exhausted. The people are in a state of despair and are resolved to risk their lives so that the next generation of Colombians will not be slaves. . . . Every sincere revolutionary has to acknowledge that armed combat is the only alternative left."

A recent publication of the National Council of Churches asked: "Is it lawful for the Christian actively to participate in revolutionary movements that may resort to violence in cases where the goal of social transformation does not appear viable by any other means but which is indispensable from the point of view of social justice and human well-being?" Once again it was indicated that violence is to be approved when there is no other way.

If there are no alternatives, however, there is no ethical dilemma; moral theorists have always taught that no one is obliged to do the impossible. And if social justice is truly impossible except through violence, men are not morally limited to futile non-violent means. Traditional ethics, to be sure, vetoes the use of "intrinsically bad" means even in the pursuit of acceptable ends. Yet, throughout history, ethicists have condoned police coercion, defensive war, and military assistance to embattled allies. Violent means have never been treated by moralists as bad just because they were violent. No doubt many contemporary ethicists condemn atomic, bacteriological, and chemical instruments of violence as inherently evil. But these are hardly the weapons used by insurgents. One therefore must ask moralists: "Why haven't you preached that revolutionary violence is good? In the light of your own principles, it has to be good because it is not intrinsically bad and it is sometimes the only option possible."

When he opts for violence, the ethical revolutionary assumes that his revolution is inevitable or "necessary." Once revolution becomes "necessary," however, it is already too late to build safeguards against absolutizing its means or against betraying the justice of the "cause" in the name of efficiency. The problem is that revolutionaries can always argue plausibly that any realistic ethic posits efficiency as a moral requirement of *good* revolutionary action. Even the Christian Gospel warns men against building a tower unless they can finish it, or starting a war unless they can see it through. Thus, ethics can provide suitable arguments to justify launching a revolution but remains powerless to impose limits on violence or to safeguard personal rights in the prolonged conduct of warfare.

If, however, the ethics of ends-and-means is rejected, determinism will nourish both the good conscience and the dilemma of decision-makers: their good conscience because they justify revolution as necessary, their dilemma because they cannot control revolution. By its very nature, revolution forces men to tread paths whose destination is unknown. Its goals change and its participants are perpetually reëducated to new truths. Perhaps one can "free the present from the past," but who will free the future from the present? How does one answer Djilas's objection that "throughout history there have been no ideal ends which were attained with non-ideal, inhumane means, just as there has been no free society which was built by slaves. Nothing so well reveals the reality and greatness of ends as the methods used to attain them. If the end must be used to condone the means, then there is something in the end itself, in its reality, which is not worthy."

Ethical purists want revolution and love simultaneously, but the two are incompatible. Revolution consists in loving a man who does not yet exist. But Camus warns that "the man who loves a living being, if he loves him truly, can only accept to die for that living being, not for a man who does not live yet." It is sheer cynicism to preach war without waging it, or peace and justice without forging the means to establish them.

Revolutionary programs impel men to action and sacrifice by denouncing the injustices they suffer in their flesh and blood. Yet, revolutionaries risk perpetrating new injustices on that very flesh in the name of an idealized man who lies at the term of history. This is why if it wishes to be human, revolution must accept moral relativity as a principle: its universe is that of relative values. Instead of saying, with Hegel and Marx, that all is necessary, it only proclaims that all is possible. And Camus adds: "At a certain point on the farthest frontier, it is worth making the supreme sacrifice for the sake of the possible."

The virtue of revolutionaries and non-revolutionaries alike resides in their choice of means, for, in the last analysis, the ends of all combatants are good. All revolutions must strive to wed power to love. The crucial question is: Will love bow in submission to power, because love is powerless to triumph in the real world? Or will power accept love's gentle yoke in recognition of its own impotence to serve human purposes? Frantz Fanon, the black theorist of the Algerian revolt, held that the exploited man can only be liberated if he uses all available means, and that of force first and foremost. Thomas Merton, on the contrary, placed his ultimate faith in the superior efficacy of love, openness, peaceful negotiation, and above all of truth. "Power always protects the good of some at the expense of all the others. Only love can attain and preserve the good of all. Any claim to build the security of *all* on force is a manifest imposture."

A commitment to one or another of these conflicting acts of faith transcends all rational discourse on the ethics of violence. In both cases the believer falls into an "ethics of distress" situation; regardless of his choice, he cannot fully predict or control the outcome of his options. Violence perpetrated on behalf of justice can become repression under the facile pretext of "eliminating counter-revolutionaries" or "saving the revolution." Non-violence practiced for love's sake just as readily paves the way for that greater violence which is born of the desperation of the oppressed. One cannot avoid risking the subversion of one's most precious moral values, and if one is lucid one's conscience is in distress. Lucidity is essential; so is advertence to the ambiguous word "necessity." Marx called class struggle a necessity, holding that even when "enlightened" exploiters carry out reforms, they unwittingly deepen class antagonism and prepare the day of ultimate violence. The history of all class societies moves ineluctably toward conflict, Marx added, and human freedom consists solely in harnessing history's dialectics ahead of history's apocalyptic deadline.

For Jacques Ellul, the French philosopher, on the other hand, necessity is the result of a failure to meet freedom's deadline and the consequent loss of moral options. Not that it is wrong to start a revolution, but once revolutionaries have burned their bridges, they have no defenses against the temptation to subordinate purity of goals to efficiency of means. The revolutionary finally is forced to echo Jesus: "He who is not with me is against me." Insurgents and counter-insurgents alike ultimately need every citizen and cannot afford to let him remain neutral. Under both kinds of necessity absolute ethical choices lose their meaning; they become impossible or superfluous.

៛

One of the problems facing revolutionaries is that the ethical implication of subversive activities has been neglected in the traditional systems. For example, there is no Christian ethic of revolution; there are only feeble attempts by Christians to salvage values in complex revolutionary situations. Many such efforts have foundered on the shoals of the theory which posits four criteria for a just war: (a) war must be declared by legitimate authority; (b) the cause must be just — this has usually been interpreted to mean self-defense or helping a beleaguered ally under attack; (c) those who wage war must preserve a right intention — their goal must remain peace not war, reconciliation not vengeance, justice not conquest; (d) only lawful means are permitted — that is, means must be morally indifferent or inherently good.

These criteria urge moderation in destruction and advocate "proportionality" between damage inflicted and benefits obtained. The principle of licit means assumes an operational difference between combatants and noncombatants, and knowledge of what constitutes a good or a bad instrument of violence.

Seeking for an ethical justification, certain Latin-American Christians have reinterpreted these principles to make them fit the revolutionary situation of their continent. Thus revised, the code reads as follows: (a) it must be certain that legitimate authority has lost its mission, that is, has become tyrannical or incapable of administering the common good;

(b) all peaceful means must be exhausted before revolutionary violence is lawful; (c) revolution's anticipated "good" effects must outweigh the evil it causes; (d) revolutionary leaders must entertain reasonable hope of success; (e) no intrinsically evil means can be employed; (f) it is forbidden to exacerbate the pre-revolutionary situation in order to precipitate the outbreak of violence.

It is not necessary to refute such an argument point by point to discover that these criteria, even refurbished to fit revolutionary situations, overlook political realities. Take the first principle—who will judge whether or not legitimate authority has lost its mission? A majority of voters? What if voters represent but a minority of citizens? A revolutionary party composed of a tiny minority? But who has given it a mandate to speak for the body politic? The masses? A particular class? Through what mechanism can these judgments be tested, according to what rules?

As for exhausting all peaceful means, what does a budding revolutionary group do if it realistically must expect to be wiped out unless it conceals its opposition to the ruling elite until ready to engage in combat at a propitious moment? And who can predict a revolution's possible "good" or "bad" effects? How does one gauge "reasonable" prospects of success? Holden Roberto's GRAE (Governo Revolucionário de Angola no Exíllio) has been fighting eight years and still seems far from victory. It took the Algerians nine years to win their battle. If we are to believe Ho Chi Minh, the revolutionary who perseveres to the end is certain to win.

Why belabor the point? The "just-war theory" is worthless; it cannot come to grips with the psychological and political realities of revolutionary situations.

What of some form of Christian situation ethics? This approach is often hardheaded. But it provides no norms other than purely subjective ones for evaluating objective situations. A man's ideology, class interests, occupational bias, heredity, and environmental conditioning, to say nothing of his personal characteristics, go far toward inclining him toward violence or non-violence. Can any genuine social conscience exist if the ultimate appeal is to subjective persuasion? At best, such a position leads to moral ambiguity. Reinhold Niebuhr was right thirty-five years ago in declaring that "the struggle for social justice in the present economic order involves the assertion of rights, the rights of the disinherited, and the use of coercion. Both are incompatible with the pure love ethic found in the Gospels. How, then, do we justify the strategy of the 'class struggle'? We simply cannot do so in purely Christian terms."

The Gospels contain no ethic of the status quo and no ethic of revolution. All ethical positions taken in political affairs compromise Jesus' "pure love" principle. Yet there is no need to assume that pure love is meant to be an ethical norm. Christianity urges the dynamics of love, but love's demands cannot adequately be expressed in juridical terms. Jesus advocates love of enemies, eschatological hope in God's defense of the victimized, and the sacrifice of one's rights for the sake of brotherhood, not as moral laws but as a spiritual ideal which constantly thrusts men beyond ethics and beyond the "realistic" dictates of political wisdom. The worst distress for a Christian is to be forced to resort to violence in his defense of human values. Distress means that he is not free to work on behalf of love without, at least temporarily, professing his inability to love, to forgive, or to transmute his earthly despair into eschatological hope. It is no weakness of Christianity or bankruptcy of the Gospel that breeds this distress; it is man's condition in history. Were man more than human he could create goodness, justice, and freedom for all men without having to destroy these values in those he calls enemies, perhaps even in himself. If man did not live in history, he could free the present from the past. Yet, no revolutionary can totally free the present from the past. Destruction never leaves the destroyer unscarred and free to build with a clear conscience.

Revolutionary situations create an ethical dilemma whose only issues are heroism or compromise. But the heroic way of Gandhi, Martin Luther King, and Danilo Dolci is too lofty for the masses. Some men will seek to escape distress by ignoring reality or by abdicating ethics, but these are pseudo-solutions. Most men cannot rise to heroism. Their duty is to avoid escapism, and if they wish to be moral they must resist the determinisms of violence or the possible complicities of non-violence. Neither violence nor non-violence can be absolute. Total non-violence is connivance with the violence of exploiters; total violence is the rationalization of historic evils.

Let us turn now to Marxism. "The worst thing that can befall a leader of an extreme party," Engels wrote in 1850, "is to be compelled to take over a government in an epoch when the movement is not yet ripe for the domination of the class which he represents, and for the realization of the measures which that domination implies. What he *can* do depends not upon his will but upon the level of development of the material means of existence, of the conditions of production and commerce upon which class contradictions always repose. What he *ought* to do, what his party demands of him, again depends not upon him or the stage of development of the class struggle and its conditions. . . . Thus he necessarily finds himself in an unsolvable dilemma. What he *can* do contradicts all his previous actions, principles, and the immediate interests of his party, and what he *ought* to do cannot be done."

As sadly as any purist Christian, Engels lamented the betrayal, not of Gospel love, but of proper class interests. Like contemporary Christians, he saw his elite in the grip of an insoluble ethical dilemma. And he defined political ethics as a function of time, the moment in the history of class struggle, and not of right objectives or lofty personal goals. He reluctantly conceded that revolutionary leaders must at times be liars and manipulate men: "Whoever is put into this awkward position is irrevocably lost!"

For Marx, violence was a necessity; using it posed no problem of principle. But times have changed. There may well be, in the words of I. F. Stone, "something anachronistic in Castro's Cuba and in Che's mission to build a new and bigger Sierra Maestra in the Andes. The hard realities of the hemisphere are very different from the revolutionary clichés of Castroism. How do you create new managerial and scientific cadres to replace the old oligarchies and American aid?" Even if one holds that the goal of guerrilla warfare is the conquest of political power, what does one do with political power after one's revolution is successful? Is the successful revolutionary, as Engels feared, simply trapped by objective conditions of history? Mobilizing the oppressed by the use of a pedagogy whose central themes are class struggle and the suppression of exploitation encourages simplistic allegiances to a dogmatism ill-prepared to be self-corrective once power has been gained. It is a dangerous fallacy for any revolutionary ethic to require its adherents to draw a blank check on their future.

To this day Djilas's query about means and ends has not been satisfactorily answered by Marxists. Some Marxists (Garaudy, Althusser, Adam Schaff, Ernst Fischer, Machovek, and others) engage in dialogue, it is true. Joint Communist/Christian groups have debated the possibility, in Marxist terms, of dissociating religious alienation from social alienation. By and large, however, Marxist ethics remains in a state of disarray and raises more questions than it can answer. China's cultural revolution, in particular, seriously undermines the assumption of all revolutionaries since 1789, that a radical act of violence will burst open the door to a better society. As one editorialist wrote (*The Economist,* January 14, 1967): "It is this belief that Chairman Mao has now finally and perhaps decisively put in doubt. . . . What is needed, and what he has set himself to achieve, is perpetual revolution — to be precise, a regular succession of upheavals, following each other at intervals of a generation or less. He believes that nothing short of this will keep the original revolutionary impetus alive." Yet Mao is charged with heresy by the Holy Office of Marxist orthodoxy and is challenged within China itself by many old Yenan revolutionary comrades. Even if Mao is proved right, as is quite possible, why should downtrodden men sacrifice their all for a revolution that must be discarded every fifteen years?

Old doctrinal certitudes are being eroded by the relativities of political life. Even that wily old Italian Communist, Togliatti, complained before his death that Communists were incapable of recognizing the new forms of alienation they had generated in their own societies.

The problem of revolutionary ethics is now facing significant groups of Americans. For, by all known general criteria, a pre-revolutionary situation exists in the United States. Large numbers of citizens seek to change the country's basic institutions. They despair of obtaining these changes through legal channels. They are sufficiently organized to constitute a political force. They are actively accelerating the polarization of opinion without which revolutions cannot get off the ground. And there is a hardening of resistance in the face of these demands.

There are two kinds of revolutionary consciousness in the United States: that of blacks, and that of youthful white radicals. Black revolutionary consciousness is very similar to that found in the Third World. American blacks are conscious of being economically and politically exploited and know that others enjoy a disproportionate share of the rewards yielded by social effort. What is worse, their self-esteem and dignity have been crushed. It is not surprising, therefore, that black militants find in the writings of anti-colonialist spokesmen like Frantz Fanon and Ho Chi Minh rich fodder for a "pedagogy of the oppressed" suited to their needs. Malcolm X formulated a political rationale for the stirrings of the black soul. By moving the debate from the arena of "civil" to that of "human" rights, and by liberating black self-expression from the "domesticated" vocabulary of religion (Christianity and Islam), Malcolm invested his people with the mantle of universal champions of justice. He ripped off the masks behind which American society basked in its good conscience. After Malcolm, whose diagnosis of the United States as racist was confirmed by the report of the President's Commission on Civil Disorders, whites can no longer dismiss James Baldwin, LeRoi Jones, and Stokely Carmichael as the voices of raucous irrationality.

The black revolutionary is almost a pure type of Camus' universal rebel. His rebellion is aimed at one who, until now, was incapable of entertaining the notion that he was an oppressor. Black revolutionaries also face ethical dilemmas, however. They must decide for which cause they will compromise, and trace out the lines beyond which they cannot compromise. The cause is clear — liberation of the black man. Nevertheless, debate continues around what form liberation should take: a separate state, a nation within a state, or some other model. The boundaries, too, are fuzzy: Martin Luther King's means are not those of Eldridge Cleaver. Notwithstanding deep and bitter divisions among black groups, advocates of non-violence and of violence increasingly acknowledge one another as "brothers." The boundary question is largely a domestic question among blacks and offers scant leverage to whites desirous of exploiting internal differences among blacks to their own advantage.

The revolutionary consciousness of young white radicals is different. Unlike anti-colonialists or oppressed groups in underdeveloped lands, white U.S. radicals are a privileged group thrashing out against an impersonal enemy which robs them of their very being. It is true that white radical students share with black dissidents a sense of powerlessness over their own destiny since they are alienated from substantive decision-making affecting their own activities and aspirations. In this respect at least, their grievances are like those of blacks. Nonetheless, the basic complaint of white revolutionaries is different. They rebel, not because they are deprived, but because of what their exploiters wish to share with them. In this sense, theirs is a metaphysical revolt: a profound rejection of what is because it chokes off what can be. It is not its past or its present that radical youth contests but its future. More precisely, it says a resounding "No" to the future society is preparing for it. Its revolutionary consciousness is no doubt profoundly sensitive to the ethical injustice of racism, poverty, war, underdevelopment. But, above all, youth is discovering that it has been declared the heir of a social fortune it does not want. This discovery has been made at the murky level of self-identity. Its central message is that men are being trodden underfoot, not by having too little, but by having too much. To use Erich Fromm's words, American youth has learned that "affluent alienation" can be as dehumanizing as "impoverished alienation."

The cause of that alienation is the irrationality of a total system each of whose parts is supremely rational. The only posture of self-defense left is revulsion: to spit out the whole mess. Ultimately, it may prove irrational to be a radical revolutionary in the United States. But this is no deterrent, since it is also irrational *not* to be a revolutionary. All depends on the matrix of rationality from which one draws his images of where reason stops and will picks up. To some extent, every revolution is fiercely voluntaristic. But in a very special sense the revolution of American youth is structurally voluntaristic: will is the only instrument it has left to challenge the Molochian voracity of a system which is exasperatingly "rational."

Although it is true, as many observers remark, that the youthful rebellion is a revolution of bored men (*acedia* now becomes a sociological category!), I do not believe that this is its most essential note. It is above all a guilt-laden revolt. Rebels can ordinarily relate their own privations to those suffered by all the underprivileged in time (history) and space (the contemporary world). Today's American youth, however, is an envied and privileged minority. This is why nothing so painfully galls a white radical than to be told by black militants that "you can afford to be against the system, because you're living off it." The very suggestion that a revolutionary is parasitical is a blow to one who seeks identification with a class which has always challenged the right of exploiters to be parasitical. The young, of course, deny that they are parasites. And, in some mysterious sense, they are right: it is those who are most "productive" in society who are the parasites, those who live off the "capital" of Western society's residual Greek wisdom, Christian personalism, and Enlightenment rationality.

Nevertheless, youthful white radicals in the United States suffer from unconscious guilt over the fact that they cannot visibly assume before the world the posture of economic self-sufficiency. It is indeed humiliating for revolutionaries to have to depend on daddy's money or on friends within the system to pay the bills. This is true even if in most cases their revolutionary activity is confined to their student years. American revolutionaries enjoy the sympathy of numerous groups throughout the world who also have a stake in the success of internal revolution in the United States. This potential foreign support is ambivalent, however, because serious breakdowns in the U.S. system could lead to military adventurism whose chief victims might be other nations.

It is sometimes imagined that the United States is a powerful and sophisticated social system with no vulnerable nerve centers. Nerve centers are points of weakness which could collapse in the face of a relatively minor assault and lead to disruption of larger parts of the system. Whatever may be the outward appearances of strength, the American Goliath has feet of clay. One needs only to recall the chaos produced in New York City by the blackout. To this day, the precise cause of the power failure has not been determined. And it could happen again. Another sign of vulnerability, trivial perhaps but suggestive nonetheless, is the incapacity of the New York Stock Exchange to handle its voluminous paperwork except by closing down periodically for a few days in order to "catch up." Besides, as bank-clearing operations and innumerable other procedures vital to the system become increasingly centralized and computerized, the possibility grows that a well-planned tactical assault on such a nerve center — conducted by men having intimate knowledge of computers and information-processing — could produce the kind of disarray on which revolutions thrive. One need not suppose, therefore, that revolution could only succeed in the United States by accident. Thus far the main factor operating in favor of the Establishment has been the profound immaturity of the revolutionaries themselves.

It is puerile to call for power and confrontation when what is needed is a politico-technological equivalent of guerrilla warfare. Confrontation and shouted demands for power are calculated to evoke responses at precisely those points where the existing system is strongest. There is nothing startling, however, about the inability of U.S. revolutionary groups to devise a valid indigenous formula of action. This has been the common difficulty faced by most revolutionary groups. Mao nearly lost his entire army before he learned that an "orthodox" popular front with the

Nationalist Kuomintang was unworkable. Even Guevara made the mistake of thinking he could export Cuba to Bolivia. U. S. revolutionists have looked to foreign models out of desperation. They have yet to find their own; and unless they do, they are easy game. The wielders of legitimacy in this country unconsciously grasp this, I believe. One wonders whether they truly consider dissent and obstruction to be a serious threat to the foundations of American political and social institutions. University administrators warn against the dangers posed by "guerrilla warfare" on campuses. But the question remains: Do they fear that the whole house of cards will come tumbling down, or simply that their own role in the game is under assault? The question is still open.

Generally speaking, white revolutionaries in the United States are unable to answer the two crucial questions: For what cause will they compromise, and where do they draw the line beyond which they will not compromise? By their own admission, the cause has not been defined: it must be born through the process itself. Furthermore, most young radicals refuse to draw a line, because they wish to be purists. There is a noble logic to their demand for absolute purity. They have too often seen revolutionary objectives pulverized in the mill of accommodation. And they simply reject the idea that one must get his hands dirty. In every combat, it is true, evil creeps in but the only respectable human decision is to refuse all compromise in advance. When one decides to keep his hands clean he will resist being swept along by the tide of circumstances and will constantly weigh, before every choice, the degree of corruption it entails. Yet most young revolutionaries are purists as regards concessions to the "system" while remaining pathetically naïve about the compromises demanded by their own revolutionary posture. However, one simply cannot dismiss the possibility that Sartre may be right and that it is in fact impossible for a revolutionary to keep his hands clean. The reason is that counter-power corrupts quite as much as power itself. And it may even corrupt absolutely.

The Italian author Guido Piovene once compared the United States to a huge digestive system. All kinds of abrasives can be introduced into it. But like the oyster it has an infinite capacity to secrete social gastric juices which transform the rough stones of dissent into smooth pearls of conformity. If this is true, or even half true, American revolutionists face an impossible task. Preëmption or co-option may turn out to be their ineluctable destiny. Whether they reject the system, drop out of it, or fight it to the death, they will be making useful contributions to its functioning. Their only role would then be to manifest to the world the troubled conscience of revolutionaries — and of counter-revolutionaries. ᵙ

Criminal Justice

DONALD McDONALD

The American system of criminal justice—from the point at which a suspect is apprehended by the police, through pre-trial and trial court proceedings, appeals, and final disposition—is not working very well, according to two judges, a former district attorney, and a sociologist who met at the Center recently. But that is virtually the only thing on which they agreed. They differed in their diagnoses of the system as well as in their prescriptions for it.

Leading the discussion of the administration of criminal justice were: Judge Warren E. Burger of the United States Court of Appeals in Washington, D.C.; Judge Walter Schaefer of the Illinois State Superior Court; Sam Dash, former district attorney of Philadelphia, now director of the Institute of Criminal Law and Procedure, Washington, D.C.; and Gresham M. Sykes, a sociologist and director of the administration of justice program at the University of Denver Law Center.

171

Judge Burger's initial statement—which criticized the adversary system of criminal justice and questioned the strength of some cornerstones of that system —became a kind of thesis around which the dialogue pivoted and developed:

"I raise this question, and I will overstate it to try to evoke a challenging response. I say that the adversary system is not the best system of criminal justice, and that there is a better way. Many of us tend to think that while our adversary system may be inefficient, it is still the best that could have been devised. I challenge that proposition. The system is certainly inefficient and wasteful. I am not sure it is the best that could be devised. The American system, up to the time of the final verdict and appeal, puts all the emphasis on techniques, devices, mechanisms. It is the most elaborate system ever devised by a society. It is so elaborate that in many places it is breaking down. It is not working."

Judge Burger explained what he meant by techniques, devices, and mechanisms. They include the presumption that the accused is innocent; the use of juries and the consequent rules regarding evidence; the right of the defendant to remain silent; the placing of the burden of proof on the prosecution.

Many of these "incidents of the adversary system," he said, were introduced after the Magna Carta and after the development of a legal profession because lawyers wanted to offset the enormous imbalance between the power of the King and his establishment on the one hand and that of the individual person on the other. "But are all these devices of the adversary system valid in today's society?" Judge Burger asked. "I heard one Supreme Court justice say in a seminar that the presumption of innocence is 'rooted in the Constitution.' Well, it may be rooted there, but you cannot find it there. I think we have been deluded by some of our own utterances. Certainly you have heard —and judges have said—that one should not convict a man out of his own mouth. The fact is that we establish responsibility and liability and we convict in all the areas of *civil* litigation out of the mouth of the defendant."

Judge Burger said that in Europe the defendant in a criminal suit is required to answer questions; if he refuses, the judges will draw unfavorable inferences, just as parents draw inferences if their children refuse to give an account of their behavior, or teachers draw inferences from the failure of their students to explain their conduct. "So I am no longer sure that the Fifth Amendment concept, in its present form and as presently applied and interpreted, has all the validity attributed to it."

The original reasons against compelling a defendant to answer have been somewhat dissipated, the judge continued. "But whenever I discuss this with some of my colleagues they are horrified. They conjure up images of the rack and the screw. I am not talking about police officers forcing accused persons to answer questions in a police station. No one, I think, would argue for that. I am talking about requiring a defendant to testify in a modern courtroom, in the presence of a neutral judge, with his lawyer present."

Judge Burger said that it is very difficult to explain the American adversary system of criminal justice to enlightened lawyers and judges in Europe. These men, he said, have as much compassion and as much concern for human dignity as we have, but they are baffled by, for example, the exclusionary rule in the American system. This rule excludes evidence if it has been obtained by a procedure that violates a statue, a regulation, or a basic Constitutional right.

The Europeans, he said, cannot understand how we can justify the exclusion of known and reliable truth from a judicial inquiry. The judge said he answers this by pointing out that ours is an adversarial rather than an inquisitional system of justice and is based on the use of provable truth rather than on truth in the abstract. But he does not think his friends have been persuaded by this explanation. "If we cannot explain our system satisfactorily to enlightened people," the judge said, "perhaps we should reëxamine some of its fundamentals."

One of the fundamentals, the jury system, was questioned by Judge Burger. He noted that use of the jury is rapidly disappearing in England, and it generally does not exist on the Continent. In America, however, fewer defendants are waiving their right to a jury in a criminal case than ever before.

Although conceding that time and money are not the only important factors, Judge Burger pointed out that "if we could eliminate the jury we would have a lot of time. In Pennsylvania, juries are waived in eighty per cent of the cases and the system works much better. You can try a case without a jury in one day that would take you a week or two weeks with a jury. Generally speaking, criminal cases with a jury take three-and-a-half times as long to try today as they did ten years ago." Much of this time is consumed in out-of-court conferences, in which the judge excuses the jury so that he may conduct a hearing on whether the lawyer has sufficiently advised his client on the admissibility of evidence, on challenges to the nature of the arrest, and on motions made during the trial. "One judge clocked his courtroom for a week," Judge Burger said. "He found that the jury was out of the room sixty per cent of the total elapsed time of the trial."

According to Judge Burger, lawyers are the biggest offenders. "When rules are made that will help the client, the lawyer comes to believe that he isn't serving his client if he doesn't try to exploit those rules. We have eager and extraordinarily bright young men going into criminal law. They make every motion in the book. It is good to have them, and there has been a lot of good effects from them. But there is also the tendency of defense lawyers today to make a 'federal case' out of every trial. . . . Defense counsel generally are clogging the system by an excess of zeal. However, I would have to say, in exculpation of the lawyer, that he is only making use of what the system has provided and therefore perhaps cannot be criticized too much."

A major cause of the defects in the American adversary system, Judge Burger said, is that the Appellate courts and the Supreme Court, in their concern for the rights of the individual, have started down a road in which each step is a logical extension of the step immediately preceding it, "but when you get to the end of that road and look back, often you find you have arrived at a place you hadn't intended to go to at all." As an example of "unlooked-for consequences," Judge Burger cited the problem of the police lineup and the defense attorney acting as monitor of that lineup. "This puts the defense attorney in an impossible position," he said. "He is called to the station as advocate for the defendant and now he is also supposed to observe and oversee the police lineup to determine whether it complies with the standard set down by the Supreme Court. If the lineup has not been properly conducted, the defense lawyer must convert himself into a witness and testify. If we follow the rule of tainted evidence, we may have prosecutors arguing that such a lawyer is a tainted witness. The Supreme Court never defined his role at the police lineup. The decision was really a terribly bad piece of work. There should be someone at the lineup to see that it is conducted properly, but it should be a neutral magistrate, not an advocate.

"The Supreme Court embarked on this ad-hoc process of rule-making about twelve years ago. I suspect that on each case on which it ruled (and I've done it myself in our court) they hoped it would be the last one, that the problem would straighten itself out, that police would learn to do things better."

Judge Burger said the Supreme Court's actions have been a "grave mistake in methodology. They have undertaken to rewrite the code of criminal procedure on a case-by-case basis, without evidence of the impact over the broad spectrum of the administration of criminal law. They have confined themselves to the needs of each particular case."

❦

Sam Dash said he is in favor of the adversary system, in favor of the Fifth Amendment rights, and in favor of the presumption of the defendant's innocence.

"We still believe today," he said, "that government is powerful and the individual is weak and that, as a result, there is an imbalance. The Fifth Amendment is built into our system to allow the defendant to remain silent, to allow him to challenge the government and require it to prove its case beyond a reasonable doubt. This still is a valuable right in our system. Once you allow the government to have the right to ask the question of the defendant, the government begins to feel it has the right to get the right answer. In no time, you get techniques of interrogation and inquisition that move not to the rack and the screw but to psychological coercion.

176

"Unless it is limited, even good government can become overzealous. I've had experience as a district attorney. I have talked with district attorneys. Most of them assume that they operate from the best of motives. Yet, very quickly, the occupational disease of the district attorney sets in: he begins to see the Constitution as an impediment to justice."

Far from criticizing defense attorneys for an excess of zeal, Mr. Dash argued that a lawyer who did not object to testimony on technical grounds might be found to have given ineffective assistance to his client and the case would be reversed by the Appellate courts.

Mr. Dash acknowledged that the court system has become so clogged that almost a travesty of justice is perpetrated, especially in misdemeanor cases, which are sometimes handled at the rate of one every two minutes. But the solution, he suggested, may lie not in diminishing the number of rules and Constitutional safeguards for the protection of the individual rights of a defendant in a criminal case, but rather in diverting from the criminal system many individuals who are technically guilty of violations of the law but who might perhaps be more successfully treated in the community than through the criminal process.

Mr. Dash described the Offender Rehabilitation Project in the District of Columbia in which social workers give defense attorneys for the poor complete background studies of their clients, plus a rehabilitation plan that may include a job or a training program for the client, services for his family, all of the information the courts need if they are to have an alternative to a jail sentence. "It quickly became evident to us," Mr. Dash said, "that if this procedure is successful for a person caught up in the system of criminal justice, it might be just as successful in helping keep these same people out of the criminal system, helping them remain in the community. This would help unclog the courts and help make for more intelligent decisions as to the handling of cases.

"We are trying to set up a system that provides friends for the poor so that they can be treated the way the rich have been treated," Mr. Dash continued. "Many a rich client has found that he, too, can be diverted out of the system of criminal justice by his lawyer. If the rich client has a psychiatric problem, for example, his lawyer will get him under the care of a psychiatrist early, then go to the prosecutor and persuade him not to go on with the case since his client is already receiving treatment. This kind of handling has not been available to the poor."

It will be difficult to make the change he advocates, Mr. Dash conceded, because the American people today live in great fear of street crimes and are less tolerant of systems that do not deal severely with the criminal. But he himself, he indicated, feels that the greatest danger to the community comes from the organized and professional criminal element rather than from the poor who fail at crime and get caught. "The American public is primarily concerned with the latter, who threaten it violently. It is with these that we have to deal and it is with these that the criminal process has been least successful. If we are going to keep our adversary system we will have to deal with fewer individuals through the criminal process and with more individuals through the community."

Mr. Dash noted that studies made by his institute in Washington indicate that the poor who fail at crime and get caught up in the system are generally non-aggressive when it comes to asserting their Constitutional rights. They do not look upon the lawyer as a friend but a representative of the enemy. They prefer to take their chances with the police officer in front of them. They adopt a servile role. They will talk freely in the hope that their punishment will be lightened. Only seven per cent of poor people in the District of Columbia who are apprehended by police and advised of their right to have a lawyer ask for a lawyer.

"What this seems to mean is that the adversary system is not, in fact, a working system," Mr. Dash concluded. "This might be something for further study: Why do individuals distrust the system of criminal justice and elect not to use it? I also raise the question why an individual, once arrested, should not be given an attorney from the very beginning and not simply be given a choice of whether or not he wants one, because that choice itself requires counsel."

č

Judge Schaefer thought that at least two aspects of criminal justice needed considerable study: punishment for crime, and the kinds of criminal conduct that prevent people from developing their full powers as persons.

"We seem to be able to think of only two kinds of punishment for crime, incarceration or the death penalty," Judge Schaefer noted. "It seems to me we do not ever think of alternative methods, those which might tend more toward rehabilitation. We have by no means exhausted the various possibilities of punishment for crime."

Judge Schaefer spoke on other aspects of criminal justice:

THE POLICE: "The police are bitterly criticized today, but we seldom read anything about the problem of the police officer. He must operate in an environment that the rest of us do not come into contact with at all. The concentrated geographical ethnic area of the ghettos is a completely unique phenomenon, characterized primarily by hostility to the police."

LAWYERS: "Criminal law is attractive to the young lawyer today. New York and Chicago law firms, in order to attract lawyers away from criminal law, are offering $12,000 to $15,000 a year to young men just out of law school. The number of lawyers is completely inadequate. In the short run, it is impossible to eliminate the public prosecutor as we have him today, but we suffer as a result of the exclusive specialization of public defenders and public prosecutors, men who either defend or prosecute and nothing else. The public prosecutor tends to get deeply entrenched."

COURTS: "We can improve the performance of our courts by having transcripts of proceedings always available. It might be worthwhile to speculate about the possibility of having video tape recordings of actual trials to be used by both lawyers and judges to determine the adequacy of judicial, prosecutorial, and defense performance."

JURIES: "There is more justification for a jury in criminal law than in civil law. But, regardless, I have grave doubts about the jury system as such. It carries within it the seeds of its own destruction. In the misdemeanor and petty offense category, it is quite unrealistic to think about the right to a trial by jury and yet the Constitution does not draw the line."

Gresham Sykes asked point-blank: "Why have a system of criminal justice at all? The system is founded on the idea that you can punish and rehabilitate people and thus control their behavior. I think both propositions are doubtful. We should think about totally different ways of handling people who break rules. Many of them should never get near the administrative apparatus of criminal justice. If you really want to stop them, they should be stopped long before they arrive at that point.

"I have been running a neighborhood law center for a year to help meet the legal needs of the poor. I am now almost completely pessimistic about such institutions being able to accomplish anything. The legal needs of the poor are overwhelming and there are not enough lawyers in the country to handle them. There will not be enough for years and years. In a recent sample we found that there is an average of three legal needs per poor family."

Although under these circumstances it is foolish to speak of solutions, Mr. Sykes said, "we now have a completely different idea; we are moving into the area of what might be called 'preventive law.' This involves things like classes in consumer buying and counseling in domestic relations (so people will not start beating each other up). We have begun to examine ways to stop crime from occurring. We can rebuild cities, for example, in a way that could make it very difficult to commit crime. We can change our transportation systems and wipe out many problems. These things may be far more effective at controlling harmful behavior than the old, old business of picking people up, applying penal sanctions, and trying to reform their moral consciousness.

"There are many other things we could do that we are not doing. Petty crimes like mugging and purse-snatching would be less likely to happen if we lighted our streets better. We can diminish the effects of drunkenness by blocking off ends of streets so drunks will not get run over, wall up alleys so they will not get mugged, stop selling wine by the glass—let them drink beer. Skid rows are disappearing in urban renewal areas, but this raises the real question: How do you take care of all the alcoholics who used to live there?"

Mr. Sykes conceded that we must continue to have a system of criminal justice but that it must be reformed and modified so that things can be done outside the system that are not now being done within the system. These reforms, in his view, must proceed apace with the moving of large areas of human behavior out from under the criminal process.

ॐ

Although the participants in the meeting were interested in the pre-trial and post-trial aspects of criminal justice (police, penological and sociological phenomena), the limitations on their time required that the discussion center on the trial process.

Judge Burger acknowledged that it was unlikely that the American adversary system would be abandoned. He hoped that some of its "rough edges" and "excesses" could be modified. Meanwhile, a "better way" to administer criminal justice can be found, he said, in one form in Britain and in another form in the northern European countries, particularly in Holland and Denmark, where, for five summers, he had had the opportunity to observe at first hand the operation of criminal justice.

BURGER: If I were a defendant and had my choice of being tried in the American system or in that of Denmark or Holland, I would take the latter. I am not sure I would prefer this if I were a professional criminal. The professional criminal prefers the American adversary system because it has many things built into it that he can exploit. In Europe, instead of a jury, there are three professional judges who try every type of case. At some lower levels and in the case of minor violations, one professional judge may try. These judges have made this their lifework. They started as magistrates and as junior judges and moved on up. They are not drawn from the practice of the law as judges are in Britain and the United States.

Some might argue that such professional judges will become hardened, calloused, insensitive. My observation has been to the contrary. I believe that they are sensitive, responsive, compassionate, and much more tolerant of human frailties than American judges. They will never send a man to prison on a first offense. It is almost unheard of in Europe to do this unless the crime is murder. For a second offense, more often than not a man gets probation, with the threat of confinement hanging over him. In the view of European judges, the threat of confinement is a greater deterrent than confinement itself. Even a third offense will frequently be treated with a probation, with more severe restrictions.

The European courts do not have our restrictive rules of evidence. An objection to a question is unheard of. Lawyers are not engaged in a personal confrontation as they are in our adversary system. In northern European countries, the system is one of inquiry instead of an accusatory-adversary method. I do not mean there is no contention. The defense lawyer works to put his client's best foot forward. But the European court is concerned to find out from everyone who has any possible connection with the case everything it can through questioning, and this includes questioning defendants. In our system we cannot ask the defendant questions unless he takes the stand voluntarily. (In California, it was once proper for the judge and prosecutor to call the jury's attention to the fact that a defendant did not testify, but the Supreme Court has now said that this undermines the purpose of the Fifth Amendment.)

The British system and ours are both adversary in the highest sense of the word. Both are accusatory, very contentious. The reason why the British system works so much better is that only a highly trained professional trial lawyer—a barrister—is permitted to try a case in a court of general jurisdiction in important criminal cases. There are only about two thousand barristers in all England but they can try a case in a fourth the time ours take. There is none of the inter-barrister wrangling or objections that we have. Also, British judges have greater power and greater professionalism. To become a judge in Britain a man must be a barrister first. Then he goes to the trial bench. And all the Appellate judges are drawn from the trial bench.

I hope I am making it clear that I do not want simply an efficient system that convicts more people. My settlement point would be the British system, which, though highly adversary, is handled entirely by skilled professionals. But beyond and apart from efficiency, I think the system in some of the northern European countries is more humane. It is fairer across the board than it is in our country. I would suppose that a system of criminal justice ought to be judged by these three questions: Is it fair? Is it humane? Is it efficient? I put efficiency last.

In our system, a trial is a traumatic experience for everybody involved—the judge, the prosecutor, the defense counsel, and most of all for the defendant, whether he be guilty or innocent. It is not anything like that in Holland or Denmark. The American system puts a premium on skill, adroitness, even trickery, on both sides.

Bear in mind that in at least one of these European countries there is not just one judge or two or even three. Initially, an inquiry judge, the magistrate, makes a preliminary exploration. The record starts getting built there. Then both sides come in and present all their evidence and this is documented. Then generally three judges examine the evidence and make findings of fact and reach a conclusion. Next, in any serious case, these findings are reviewed in turn by either three or five Appellate judges. So, a case may involve as many as seven or nine professional judges, and all of them, I think, are disinterested, trained, and humane men.

GERALD GOTTLIEB (Center Consultant): There are two reasons why a defendant should be permitted to remain silent. One is that if he testifies he may do so ineffectively and if he is found guilty the judge may conclude that he has also committed perjury and will impose a sentence heavier than he might otherwise have imposed. The other reason is based on the fact that no person is guilty alone; he is guilty because he lives in a defective society. So until we can consider all the factors and until we have relieved some judges of a certain conceit and until we refuse to attribute to judges more wisdom that we should, the adversary system and its protections ought to be given up only very reluctantly.

BURGER: In the civil law system in Europe, they never let one judge do anything. So if one judge in three is defective, which is probably about par for the American system, there are in Denmark or Holland or Sweden two other judges to offset him.

GOTTLIEB: In our system, we have twelve to offset him. We have the jury.

SCHAEFER: What bothers me is that almost never do we have a genuine issue of guilt or innocence today. The system has so changed that what we are doing in the courtroom is trying the conduct of the police and that of the prosecutor all along the line. Has there been a misstep at this point? at that point? You know very well that the man is guilty; there is no doubt about the proof. But you must ask, for example: Was there something technically wrong with the arrest? You're always trying something irrelevant. The case is determined on something that really hasn't anything to do with guilt or innocence. To the extent you are doing that to preserve other significant values, I think it is unobjectionable and must be accepted. But with a great many derailing factors there is either no moral justification or only a very minimal justification. I have never been able to understand any ethical basis for the privilege against self-incrimination as presently applied. Initially, this did not mean that no inference may be drawn if a defendant invoked the privilege not to testify. But even assuming it always meant that, now one must forget this dominant fact in the case. I do not see any real value that is being protected.

DASH: It is true that in most cases that you review guilt is not the matter in question but there are other values you are preserving. My suggestion is that unless you preserve those other values, then what has been essentially and historically true—that is, the convicting of only guilty people—may not continue to be true. These values are important because they have required the police to act in a certain way and the prosecutor to act in a certain way. Precisely because these people are required to act in that "certain way," they are now primarily dealing with guilty people. If you no longer insist on those values, then the system gets sloppy; police officers will bring in more not-so-guilty people. We don't maintain the privilege against self-incrimination and the presumption of innocence and all these burdens in order to protect guilty people but to make sure that only guilty people get into the criminal process. I think a free and democratic society wants to become involved with the police system as little as possible.

BURGER: The whole British experience is a massive piece of evidence to support Judge Schaefer's argument. The accusatory-adversary system is practiced at its highest form in the English courts with highly contentious advocates. It has all the contention and controversy you want. But they do not add all these extra layers that have impeded our system.

DASH: The Supreme Court waited a long time in this country to see whether the police would behave in a way that would not produce illegal searches and seizures. It really prefers not to rule in many kinds of cases. But finally, acting in desperation, it has given us the kinds of rules which seem at times ridiculous but which are the only rules that can preserve the system.

BURGER: Mr. Dash suggested earlier that a jury is imperative to defend a man against excessive government power. I agree to a large extent. But a government bent on destroying individual liberties can do it with a jury or with a non-jury inquiry system. You can juggle any system if you've got enough power in the establishment to do it.

SYKES: As a sociologist, I am struck by the fact that our society has developed two great systems for discovery of truth. One of them is science, the other is law through the trial system. According to Robert Merton, there are three guiding norms of science which make the scientific ethos. They are impersonal standards of proof rather than reliance on authority, free communication of findings, and suspension of final judgment until all the facts are in, so that an issue may be reopened and reëxamined at any time. I am fascinated by the extent to which the law violates every canon of this scientific ethos. In a very significant sense, one cannot suspend judgment in a criminal trial, one must come to a decision. Decisions of not guilty cannot be reopened. The system is divided into partisans, for and against, supervised by a sort of umpire. There is no free communication of facts; there are all sorts of limitations on the use of evidence. I suspect that the legal system is not, in a way, interested in the truth. Our discussion has gone on as though law tried to separate the innocent from the guilty. I do not believe that is what the court is trying to do. I think it is trying to decide what to do with people who are guilty.

WILLIAM GORMAN (Center Fellow): Law and science are not answering the same question. Science answers the question: What is the case about something here? Law answers the question: What ought to be done? The latter rests on certain inquiries about what has been the case, what has happened.

SYKES: Law and science come together in this question: What is truth?

GORMAN: Even then, there is a difference in object-matter. For most of the natural sciences, the object-matter has a kind of necessity or near necessity to it which does not occur in human affairs because human affairs get complicated and are contingent.

DASH: One of the reasons we have set up the adversary system and why we have the burden of proof on the prosecution is our assumption that even a good district attorney might become excessive. Therefore we do not leave it to him alone to make a scientific and objective inquiry into truth because we do not believe that that is the way he will proceed.

SYKES: I think others share with me the feeling that we are in danger of moving into a totalitarian regime in our society. If I thought we were moving toward a more democratic society in this country, I would say, yes, we can get rid of some of the refinements of the judicial process. But I think we are at a different and more dangerous point and I am not willing to give up these safeguards.

BURGER: But take the city of Washington, D.C., after the riots. Store owners were arming themselves and deciding to furnish their own protection because the system of justice was not working for them. They are approaching a vigilante system, taking the law into their own hands (and they have a pretty good case of self-defense). But do we want them trying to be their own enforcers? If the system of criminal justice is working right, at least ninety per cent of the people charged with criminal acts are probably guilty of something even if not necessarily the particular act charged—because in such a system the prosecutor does his work honestly. He is not going around indicting people just for the fun of it. In that system, eighty-five to ninety per cent of the persons charged plead guilty. But as soon as you decrease that percentage substantially you get almost a breakdown of the structure of the courts. In Washington, those pleading guilty have dropped as low as sixty per cent.

The atmosphere in the country today is that it is easy to "beat the rap." The Appellate courts will take care of you if you get caught in the trial courts; some "gimmick" will come along. It is not true that this happens very often, but it is the impression that emerges in the community because people see cases,

like the Chessman case in California, tried and re-
tried; a case can go on for ten years. The things that
worry Mr. Sykes, the trend to a totalitarian rather
than a democratic society, are being brought about
precisely because of this situation. Look at the disorders in Paris. It took stern measures by President
de Gaulle to stop them. But I think all of us would
describe those measures as undemocratic—surround-
ing Paris with tanks and calling up thirty thousand
troops. Washington could be a peaceful place if we
had thirty thousand policemen stationed there, but
I wouldn't want to live in a city with thirty thousand
policemen stationed in it.

The city of Washington, with 800,000 or so people,
has more criminal homicides per year than does all
of England with its sixty million people. I am satisfied
that one of the reasons for this is that every homicide
case in our country is a long-drawn-out affair—three,
five, six, nine, eleven years. It loses its deterrent punch.
In England, you do not have cases—homicide or otherwise—tried six times. But that is a regular occurrence
in the courts of the District of Columbia. There must
be some connection between the fact that we have
180 to 190 homicides in Washington per year and the
fact that England has fewer than that in its entire
country and that Sweden, with eight million people,
has twenty homicides in a year. ❧

AUDIO TAPES:

404. ON CHINA
Although the People's Republic of China refused to send a representative to *Pacem in Terris II* Convocation, its view is forcefully expressed by Paul T. K. Lin, associate professor of history at McGill University in Canada. Depending on the listener's own point of view, this was the most effective or most detested speech of the Convocation. (29:42)

435. "I SHALL DIE BUT THAT IS ALL I SHALL DO FOR DEATH"
The late Rev. Martin Luther King, Jr., James Farmer of CORE, and Bishop C. Edward Crowther join in a stirring call for an end to genocide at home and abroad. (14:34)

482. "SUPPOSE THEY GAVE A WAR AND NO ONE CAME?"
We have all of us become so precocious about world affairs that simple solutions escape us. Thus, myth-laden fears already outdated in the nineteenth century continue in the twentieth to shape policy for the twenty-first. Justice William O. Douglas is joined by Senator J. W. Fulbright and others in a plea for simple first steps for peace that have the disarming directness and wisdom of the Sandburg lines which give this tape its title. (29:46)

253. IS HISTORY OUT OF CONTROL?
Historically, in wartime more people have died from famine and disease than from weapons. Now for the first time the prospect is reversed. Yet man, the most adaptable of all the animal species, appears unable to change swiftly enough to adapt to this new phase in our culture, which requires a world without war. A talk by Dr. Jerome Frank, professor of psychiatry at Johns Hopkins University, followed by a lively exchange with Robert M. Hutchins. (44:57)

A complete listing of Center tapes is available free upon request.
Tapes, which are on five-inch reels, 3¾ ips, half-track, and also available on cassettes, may be ordered at $7.50 each from the Center, Box 4068, Santa Barbara, California 93103. (California residents add 5% sales tax.)

PUBLICATIONS:

A complete catalogue of previously published Center materials
is also made available at no charge from the Center,
Box 4068, Santa Barbara, California 93103.